GUNS AND BUGLES

The Story of the 6th Bn K.S.L.I - 181st Field Regiment R.A.

1940 - 1946

GUNS AND BUGLES

The Story of the 6th Bn K.S.L.I - 181st Field Regiment R.A.

1940 - 1946

Don Neal

To Alan
Best Wishes
Don Neal
1·12·01

Brewin Books

First published by Brewin Books Ltd,
56 Alcester Road, Studley,
Warwickshire B80 7LG in 2001
www.brewinbooks.com

ISBN 1 85858 192 3

A Cataloguing in Publication Record
for this title is available from
the British Library.

Typeset in Times
Printed in Great Britain
by Warwick Printing Company Limited,

TABLE OF CONTENTS

The following pictures appear between pages 14 and 15

X.   *Officers 178 Bty, Rear: 2/Lt McLeod, Lt. Clements, Lt Buchanan, Lt Jones, 2/Lt Todd. Front: Capt Meredith, Capt Martin, Maj Moorshead, Capt Shaw, Lt Trewby.*

Officers 179 Bty, Rear: Lt Mulholland, Lt Jones, Lt Hewitt, Lt Murray, Lt Boyd, Lt Porter. Front: Capt Prutton, Capt Bristow, Maj Sedgwick, Capt Attewell.

XI.   *C Troop, June 1944. Rear: Bdr Hall, Bdr Forknall, Bdr Edwards, U/K, Balcombe, U/K, Willey, Sig Smith 63, Lewis, U/K, Adams, Smith 88.*
Row 3: Gnr Neal, Dvr McInery, Fox, Basnett, U/K, Dvr Compton, U/K, Ball, Scott, May, U/K, U/K, Bryant, Smith. Row 2: Evans 33, Parsons, Dvr Cotton, Barnes, Sig Abbiss, U/K, Sig Whittingham, Sig Broomhall, Sig Adams, U/K, Sig Huyton, Sig Woods, Edwards, Sig Briathwaite, Hassle, Bdr Furlough. Front: Bdr Dalton, Bdr Kilby, Sgt Mottram, Sgt Darby, BSM Cook, Lt Clements, Capt Meredith, 2/Lt Todd, Sgt Gunn, Sgt Powell, Sgt Packer, Bdr Aspley, L/Sgt Eden.

XII.   *HQ 181 Field Regt. RA, Ridley Hall, June 1944. Rgtl HQ. June 1944, Rear: U/K, U/K, Bty Clerk, U/K, U/K Bdr Cook, U/K, U/K, U/K, U/K, Sig Jones, U/K, Bdr Bennet, Dvr King, Dvr Kendrew, Evans, Dvr Snooks, Devaney. Row 3: U/K, U/K, Dvr Spence, Sig Garvey, U/K, U/K, Sig Billingham, U/K, U/K, Bdr Evans, L/Bdr Ashton, Dvr Tapperal, U/K, U/K, Jones, Evans. Row 2: U/K Sig, U/K Dvr, Sig Chamberlain, U/K, Dvr Garland, U/K, Dvr Hall, U/K, Sig Symes, Brown, Clewes, Forrest, Dvr Clerk. Front: Pye, Bdr George, Lucas, U/K, U/K Cook, Dvr Ingeson, BQMS Norcross, Capt Trewby, Lt Mcloed, BSM Norton, Sgt Hunt, Bdr Marsden, Snape, Owen.*

XIII.   *D Troop Ridley Hall June 1944, Rear: U/K, U/K, U/K, Watson, Bennall, Mills. Row 3: Hartshorne, U/K, Prince, Jones, U/K, U/K, Wall, U/K, U/K, Fisher, Fellows, Daffern, U/K, U/K, U/K, U/K, Gwatkin. Row 2: Parsons, Kirk, Poutney, Clarke, U/K, U/K, U/K, Tudor, U/K, U/K, U/K, Beardsmore, Cuff, U/K, U/K. Front Row: Drake, Jinks, Hyde, U/K, Sgt Foster, Sgt Guy, Sgt Leighton, Lt Jones, Capt Shaw, Lt Buchanan, BSM Oliver, Sgt Layton, Sgt Holdsworth, Bdr Clark, Bdr Griffiths. Seated: Lacey, Turvey, Maddox, Morriss, Evans, Williams.*

XIV.   *B Troop 177 Bty 2nd June 1944. Back Row: Gnrs Pugh, Bramald, Daltry, Godfrey, Bowell, Baker, Goy, Todd, Andrews, Gordon, L/Bdr Moyle.*
Row 4: Gnrs Coley, Geeson, Hughes, Dimmock, Stevens, Cummings, Hamilton, Pardoe, Husband, Jones, Bates. Row 3 Gnrs Cartwright, Gregory, Houlgrave, Punton, Clapham, Roberts, Brook, Pick, Berrick, Fitzmaurice, James 70, Lewis, Douglas, Kelso. Row 2: Bdrs Saddler, Hopper, Luke, Sgts Fletcher, Bull, BSM Clacker, Lt McOwen, Capt Cory-Wright, Lt Stokes, Sgts Desborough, Winter, Sturley, Clee, Bdrs Bugler, Crouch. Front Row: Gnrs Pendlebury, Marlow, Griffiths, McDonald, Tighe, Jennings, James 96, Kinsey, Wood. Absent: Stokoe, Neville, Laycock.

XV.   *HQ positions. 1940 - 1942.*

XVI.   *Route covered by the Shrewsbury Marches, Jan/Feb 1942.*

The following pictures appear between pages 46 and 47

page

XVII. *Three unknown soldiers relax in dugouts between fighting. Guns ready for action in the background. Note rifle stack on right.*

FOP near Ueltzen April 1945, F/Ground, Sgt Telfer (6KOSB) B/Ground, Gnrs Mountford, Jenks. Note Sgt Telfers Sten Gun.

XVIII. *Fop Team 177 Bty April 1945, Rear: Gnrs Hogg, Goddard, Major Browne Front: Gnrs Richardson, Ballymont, Sgt Jennings.*

CP Team 177 Bty Nr Artlingen, L/R Capt Stokes, L/Bdr Watts, Gnrs Holmes, Vincash (with sten gun) Jones, Palmer, Hambleton, Richardson. Ready for grub!

XIX. *Digging Gun Pits, L/R BSM Oliver, U/K, Sgt Layton, Lt Mitchell, L/Bdr Newall, U/K. Just outside Vynen - Vynen church steeple in the background.*

In action! - 178 Bty. East bank of the Rhine 25th March 1945.

XX. *L/Bdr. Howarth – L/Bdr. Westwood – L/Bdr. Winkle*
L/Bdr. Dodd – Unknown L/Sgt. - L/Cpl. Freddie Poole
Lt. David 'Sam' Small – Lt. Wladyslaw Rolski Polish Interpreter –
Lt. Angus McLeod

XXI. *Bdr. 'Pinkie' Fisher – Lt. DFA Trewby – Capt. George Easter*
Capt. Moss Walters – Capt. Nigel Prutton – Capt. Ray Bristowe
Unknown – Brig. E.O. Herbert & Gen.Omar Bradley

XXII. *Capt. A.J.J. Cory-Wright – Unknown Bdr. – Bdr. Jones*
Bdr. Brooker – Bdr. George Aspley MM – Bdr. Griffin
Bdr. H. (Ginger) Forknall – Bdr. Moore – Unknown Bdr.

XXIII. *Unknown Gnr. – Gnr. Cartwright – Gnr-Dvr. Handby*
Gnr-Sig. Horton – Gnr. Wain – Gnr. Jervis
Gnr. Rees – Gnr. Walker 21 – Gnr. Walker 21

XXIV. *Gnr-Dvr. Canta – Gnr-Dvr. Harold – Gnr-Dvr. MacDonald*
Gnr-Dvr. Wakely – Gnr-Sig. Harding – Gnr. Harris
Gnr. Sam Hassal – Unknown Gnr. – Gnr. Timmins

XXV. *Lt. Ron Foulds – Maj. John Robertson – Rose*
Sgt. E. Mottram – Sgt. E.W. (Ted) Packer – Sgt. Fred Darby
Sgt. George Cowern – Gnr. George Neal C Troop – Gnr. Frank Foster D Troop

XXVI. *Officers Mess 178 Bty Breitenfelde 1945, Rear: 2/Lt Rwiatowski, Lt Foulds, Lt McLeod, Lt Mitchell, Lt Gow, Capt Ducquenoy.Front: Capt Meredith MC, Capt Sharpe, Maj Grahame, Capt Shaw DSO, Capt Trewby.*

The following pictures appear between pages 78 and 79

ACKNOWLEDGEMENTS

I have been working on this project for some six years in total and during that time I have had help from many sources; small bits of information often came my way fleetingly, but the majority of it was gleaned through letters and interviews from the men who were there, old now, many of them now in their eighties. Sadly since the beginning, five old soldiers have passed on. This is the most important reason why stories like this should be told.

A particular thankyou must go to David Gimes. When I came to this project my knowledge of things military was scant and disjointed. His knowledge has been invaluable, he has patiently guided me through military jargon and terminology, teaching me much along the way and has always been a great supporter.

Very often I have written to an old address, and through a vigilant, caring postman my letter has found its mark. I have on occasions, of course, written to people who have long since died, my enquiries having then been answered by a close relative, a brother or sister, son or daughter who took the trouble, and trusted me with treasured photos and letters which they allowed me to copy. All of them helped me to a greater or lesser degree in some way and the roll is in alphabetical order. Without the co-operation and support from the following, this task would have only been half complete.

L/Bdr. C.	Ashton*	Major ADG.	Shaw DSO.	Mr. D.	Gimes
Mr. D.	Buxton	Lt. D.	Small	Fus. H.	Holder
Mr. P.	Duckers MA	Miss. L & AB.	Smith	Mr. W.	Meredith
L/Sgt.	EW. Eden	Capt. TJ.	Stokes	Bdr. F.	Parsons
Sgt. G.	Gibbons	Mrs. M.	Webster	Capt. JD.	Shaw
Mrs. M.	Greenwood	Mrs. S.	Wayman	Gnr. C.	Spence
Gnr. P.	Lewis*	Sgt. F.	Darby*	Lt. J. H.	Thomlinson
Gnr. J.	May	Mr. G.	Bourne	Capt. MJ.	Walters*
Capt. P.	Mulholland	Major WM.	Busby	Major JHH.	York MBE.
B & W	Printers	Mrs. V.	Read		

Since died.

I would also like to thank the staff of the: Imperial War Museum, Commonwealth War Graves Commission, Ministry of Defence, Public Record Office, Kew, Regimental Museum KSLI, The Silver Bugle and The Royal Artillery Institute

Extracts from War Diaries   P.R.O. WO 171/1000/4854/4197 : WO166/7064
Extracts from Recommendations   P.R.O. WO 373/51

**To my Dad - Who was always there
and to the Officers and men of
6KSLI / 181 Field Regt. R.A.**

I have made every effort to report facts and events as accurately as possible as they were related to me by the ex-soldiers I talked and wrote to. Obviously the passage of time plays tricks with the memory and on occasions I heard different versions of the same story. One thing that every one agreed on was the hardship the men suffered, often going without sleep and eating a poor diet for many days on end. In particular during the time spent waiting to cross the River Mass, when the men spent weeks in trenches and it rained almost non-stop the whole time. Add to this the stress of coming under attack by air, enemy Artillery and Armour on an almost daily basis then it is small wonder that many of the men who fought were glad to put the war behind them. I would be delighted to hear from any men who were part of, either the 6th Bn. KSLI or the 181st Field Regt. or indeed any of the men who fought with the 15th Scottish Div.

Don Neal

website: www.gunsandbugles.com • email: don@gunsandbugles.com

Cover Photos:
Top - Bren Carrier team - 6th Bn. KSLI
Left to Right: L/Cpl. C. Ashton, L/Cpl. E. George, Sgt. C. Bourne, Pte. W. Sanbrook
Bottom - L/Bdr A. Smith and Gnr G. Neal
Left to Right: L/Bdr. A. Smith, Gnr. G. Neal

FOREWORD
Major A.D.G. Shaw DSO R.A. (retd)

Since the end of the Second World War there have been many changes to the Military establishment, and many famous and historic Regiments have disappeared in all but name. It is important therefore that their histories should be recorded as fully as possible, and their names and deeds be perpetuated. The 6th Bn. King's Shropshire Light Infantry suffered in as much that it never completed its existence as such, it being converted to a Field Artillery unit. This is an excellent effort by Don Neal some 50 odd years later to put together the story of the 6th Bn. and its successor, the 181st Field Regiment RA. His research over a period of six years, sifting through official records, endless pages of documents, personal interviews, and correspondence has produced a very coherent and moving record, brought to life by a collection of excellent photographs. A fitting tribute to his Father and the four hundred plus men of Shropshire and the surrounding counties, who merged with three hundred or so Artillerymen to produce a Field Regiment in the very best traditions of the Royal Regiment of Artillery. The 181st Field Regiment was fortunate to be affiliated to the 15th Scottish Division, where it found itself amongst soldiers and Regiments of great tradition and pride in their own histories. This encouraged the men of the 181st to rise to the highest possible level of achievement. It was also of great credit to the men that they should be so readily accepted by the 'Jocks' to such an extent that by the end of the War they were not referred to as the 'Gunners' but as 'Our Gunners' such was the affection and esteem shown by the men of the Scottish Infantry.

PREFACE
Major J.H.H. York MBE B.A.

Mr Donald G Neal's chronicle of the World War II campaign service of 6th Battalion The King's Shropshire Light Infantry is the rewarding result of a great deal of meticulous research by its author, inspired by his father's war service in 6KSLI and 181St Field Regiment Royal Artillery.

This fascinating account of a Battalion which, remarkably and most successfully, converted from an Infantry to a Field Artillery role in the middle of a major war fills the last major gap in the 1939-45 archives of the KSLI. The Regiment will long be indebted to the author for producing a book which is not only of great historical interest but which also pays fitting tribute to the courage, steadfastness and loyalty of the Shropshire Soldier in war.

INTRODUCTION

My Father died in 1990. He hardly ever mentioned the war or his part in it, I knew he was in the Royal Artillery, and that he enjoyed his army service. His military conduct was described as exemplary, and he was given a glowing testimonial by his Battery Commander. He was well organised, methodical, with an attention to detail; All habits that he probably picked up in the army. Occasionally in sympathetic company, usually another old soldier, one or two stories would surface and I would have a glimpse of his experience. One in particular concerned the deaths of three young lads, bearing in mind that at the time Dad was 30 years old.

These three had been detailed to take spare radio parts to a Forward Observation Post, and were all killed. Their bodies were recovered during the night by a party of volunteers, which included my Dad, all led by (Sgt.) Dick Fletcher, described as an 'an old sweat' by Dad. This story always tailed off with an embarrassing show of emotion, so I guessed that he must have had a few bad memories to live with. Since my project began I have learned the details of this incident and spoken to some of the men who were there, and it was indeed a very sad episode for ' Charlie Troop'. The events were recorded at the time by Dick Fletcher in his diary which I have transcribed, and included in my account. Dick died in 1991 and although I never had the chance to meet him, I have met his Daughter, Mrs. Val Read, who was kind enough to let me look through her Fathers mementoes and photographs.

Like many of the men who fought in the last war, Dad never bothered to apply for his Campaign Medals preferring to put the war behind him. I had already inherited my Grandfather's medals from the Great War (by coincidence he too was an Artilleryman) so, on a whim I decided to send for Dad's Medals; that was in 1976. I kept them in a drawer, and on occasions when I got them out to show someone, they would invariably ask what he did in the war, of course I didn't know. My story moves on some twenty years, to 1995 when I met someone through business who told me that he was a military researcher. My interest in research had already been fired during the previous ten years which I had spent tracing my family history. My associate Dave Buxton suggested that I send for my Dad's service record. After the usual formalities it arrived. The military jargon was soon explained to me by Dave, who pointed out the connection with the King's Shropshire Light Infantry.

He was to put me in touch with a friend of his, who he said was an authority on all things KSLI and would be interested in speaking to me. David Gimes guided me through the service record, and later produced a photocopy of two articles that had been published in the Regimental Journal in 1958. These had been written by two ex-Officers, one of them, my Dad's old Troop Commander Major John Meredith. Included in the article was mention of a number of his ex-Troop members, and I was thrilled to see that my Dad's name was included. From this point, with help from David Gimes, I was determined to find out what my Dad had 'done in the war'.

4040028 Gnr. George Henry Neal - Enlisted into the 6th Bn. KSLI on 17th July 1940,
Later posted to C Troop 181 Field Regiment RA.

Chapter One

6TH BATTALION KING'S SHROPSHIRE LIGHT INFANTRY FORMATION 1940

I failed to find an army order for the date of formation of the 6th Bn. KSLI. A news report in the Daily Express, dated 1945, puts a precise date of 5th June 1940; another, from an unknown newspaper clipping tells us it was soon after Dunkirk which is about the same. The Army List indicates that the first C.O., Lt.Col RBS Munn MC, was promoted T/Lt. Col on 4/10/1940. However the Battalion was certainly formed well before this date, as there were two large intakes of men on 24th and 27th June. These intakes were continuous throughout July with three large drafts of men arriving on the 17th, 24th, and 27th. The final recruits arrived in early August. No doubt these early Conscripts must have been shaped by a core of Regular and ex-Regular Officers and NCO's. The Battalion War Diary did not start until September 1940, and so the early days have been put together by one of the first to arrive, Charlie Ashton, a Brummie who fortunately lived close by. He was one of my first contacts, through a local newspaper appeal, and sadly passed away before my account was finished. I spent many hours with him, and he confessed that after 50 odd years he had talked about his war more to me than anyone. During the interview the hardships and harrowing experiences that the men had endured became apparent. Charlie took a water carrier into a Concentration Camp at Celle, an experience he did not want to recall. We took many pauses while he regained his composure. He was instructed to report to the Depot in Shrewsbury and from there the first to arrive were billeted in The Maltings - an outstation of the Depot, at Ditherington.

By the beginning of July the new Battalion had moved to North Allerton in Nottinghamshire and was formed into four Companies, unusually lettered W, X, Y, and Z. It continued to take further enlistments, Most of the men came from Shropshire, Herefordshire, Staffordshire the Welsh border and the Midlands. It was here that it came to full strength to begin its basic training in and around Sherwood Forest. The Battalion HQ was at Thoresby Park and the first Commanding Officer, Lt.Col RBS Munn, a Great War KSLI veteran who had distinguished himself winning a Military Cross. He soon became known as 'Mad Munn' amongst both Officers and men. The men were living under canvas, in tents which held eight men, one of them a Regular Cpl. teaching the ways of the Army; for many it would be the first time they had been away from home. The youngest would be 18 years old, and no doubt for them it was a great adventure whilst for others, like my Dad, who was 27 at the time, married with a child, they would be leaving their wives and families behind.

That Summer was very dry, which was a mixed blessing for the new recruits, as one of them recalled, constantly having to clean their kit as the dust got into every nook and cranny. During this time they would be learning how to drill properly, look after their kit, and be able to distinguish the difference and meaning of about sixteen bugle calls which would wake them up in the morning, summon them for food, post, and a dozen other things before putting them to bed at the end of the day. Fortunately these new recruits did not have to suffer the indignity of having to 'drill' in their civvies using broomsticks for rifles, as did many new recruits from other Regiments I have spoken to at that time! They were kitted out in the new pattern khaki battledress and webbing and armed with the standard issue Lee Enfield rifle, though I have photos with one or two men, who may have been Regulars, wearing the old pre-1939 uniform reminding one of the soldiers from a previous war. The stiff S.D.(service dress) cap was worn in the early days but these were phased out in favour of the more practical and familiar F.S.(field service) cap. *To be worn on parade, with the point over the bridge of the nose*, an order almost totally ignored once the men got outside camp, as many Photo's will testify. The men much preferred wearing them at a jaunty angle on the side of the head where they almost defied gravity in staying on. The men were also allowed to purchase an identical cap in Infantry Green for walking out only. The 6th Bn. had its own regimental shoulder title, in red lettering on a dark green background, "THE KING'S SHROPSHIRE L.I." Although I had known the title for some time, none of my old soldiers could recall the colours. It was almost two years before I came across my one and only example, once worn by Major John Meredith. The reason for this, will be explained more fully later, when the Battalion became a Royal Artillery unit, and because of a shortage of R.A. insignia the men were instructed to remove the words KINGS and L.I. (leaving the word SHROPSHIRE) so it is reasonable to assume that almost all of the original issue were altered. I am pleased to say that I have an example of an 'altered' title once worn by L/Bdr. Albert Smith.

It was the 1st September before the Adjutant started to complete the daily task of compiling the Regimental Diary and the very first entry reads: *Bn. strength, 30 Officers and 947 O.R's*. These were 95% conscripted men . Battalion HQ had moved to Wellbeck Abbey just a short move from Thoresby Park. Amongst the early recruits, and remembered by everyone was a stable of greyhounds!! Officially regarded as mascots (in the loosest sense) and brought to the Battalion by the C/O whose love of gambling was second only to his love of discipline, he also encouraged any soldiers who were interested to keep their own dogs. Cpl Andy Mullan was known to have kept and raced at least four. Major Dudley Shaw remembers there being well over twenty at one time. Meetings were held regularly and recorded in the Regimental Diary, the first on the 14th Sept 1940. *In the Abbeygrounds - it was a great success, about £10 was made towards Regimental funds*. Brig. A.H. Hopwood attended! No secret were these meetings, If there was no suitable track then the men were detailed to prepare one, and on race days - *'All ranks must attend'* A further two meetings were held before the Battalion moved to duties on the East Coast, one drawing a crowd of about 2,000 people! *All money to Bn. Comfort fund*. The Battalion's first Christmas arrived and Y Coy won the cigarettes for the best decorated billets and, *the men had a wonderful Christmas dinner prepared by the Officers, and the WO's and Sgt's waited on the tables*. Immediately after Christmas the Battalion moved to the Lincolnshire coast.

Chapter Two

HOME DEFENCE LINCOLNSHIRE COAST 1941-1942

After six month's initial training the 6th Bn. KSLI was to be posted on coastal defence. The move to Boston took place on 12th January 1941 and by the 14th, Battalion HQ. was installed at Wangley Manor a position just south of Skegness in Lincolnshire. Here they came under command of 204th Infantry Brigade (Home) Northern Command. The men would now be wearing the cloth badge of the Brigade on their upper sleeve. This was a blue triangle with three triangles within, representing the colours of the Brigades three senior Battalions the 7th and 8th Bn's. South Lancs.Regt, the 12th Bn. Sherwood Foresters, and the 7th Bn. Leics Regt. Together they would be defending a length of coastline between Mablethorpe in the North and Ingoldmells Point in the South, a distance of some 27 Miles. This would involve maintaining and patrolling the forward defence lines and anti-tank devices, and also included regular tours of duty guarding local air bases. Parties of men were also sent to help on local farms. Time was also spent taking part in regular exercises, which would improve movement co-ordination and inter battalion communications and field craft. The 6th Bn. had already been keeping up Regimental tradition, being congratulated on several occasions by Brigade on its smart turnout. Very little of the real war was evident on the east coast as the men waited in readiness for the expected German invasion, and were looking forward to having a crack at the enemy although, the sound of war was well within earshot as the the men could hear the bombing of the Midlands. This was an anxious time as many of them had families in that area, and facilities were arranged for them to be kept informed of the situation. Occasionally, bombs were also dropped locally inland, more by accident than design, and on one occasion, when a returning bomber dropped its unused bombs, its crew would have been pleased to know that they almost wiped out Battalion HQ. 6 KSLI. L/Cpl Charlie Ashton was having a shave at the time when the roof of his billet was blown off and (Capt)Bill Busby remembers it very well. He was in BHQ at the time (local hotel) with the C/O, Basil Munn. Also present was Basil's brother, Major LS Munn, an officer in the Battalion who, when he heard the bombs falling so close promptly dived under the table. Basil was so embarrassed that he had his brother re-posted the next day! The Busby Family was well known in the Regiment. Bill's grandfather, father, and two brothers all served with the Regiment I'm pleased to say that Bill is living in happy retirement on the Isle of Wight, now well into his 80's.

On one occasion, one of the returning enemy bombers crash landed near the Hornecastle Rd, in the Battalion's area. The incident is recorded on an hourly basis in the War Diary. Mr. Moore with 6 OR's, was dispatched to the scene, where they arrested Oberleutnant Rinck, Oberfeldwebel Ruther, Unteroffizier Wissing, and Obergefreiter Stills, who were taken to the guardroom, whilst a guard was mounted on the crashed Junkers 88. Their equipment was reported as '*extremely good*' and their morale '*100%*'. Of course everyone went down to the guard room to take a look at the dreaded Hun. The following day after interrogation they were handed over for disposal to No.10 POW camp, and escorted by Lt. Corbett and 7 OR's. The greyhound racing continued, though their number was reduced on a couple of occasions as the diary reports: '*mine exploded in forward area, greyhound jumped perimeter fence.*' Sport was a big feature, both to keep the men fit and as entertainment. The 6th Bn. had a particularly strong football team which was only beaten on one occasion, this included a game against Notts Forrest. The team featured several professional and semi-professional players. Amongst them, Bill Tudor a Welsh Schoolboy international and first team player for West Bromwich Albion, and Wrexham, Albert Titley another Albion player, Franklin of Blackpool, J. Lilley of Birmingham City, and probably the most well known, Fred Mills of Leeds Utd. who was killed in action in Holland. The boxing team also excelled itself with a very strong line up, amongst them professional Middleweight, Percy Lewis and L/Cpl. Ted Eden, who, though not a professional boxer went on to become 15th(S)Division Light-Heavyweight Champion. Ted was a skilled butcher and he helped to keep the Battery well fed in the North - West Europe Campaign, one of his first tasks was to prepare five calves for the pot. I'm pleased to say at the time of writing that Ted, now an octogenarian is living in the village of Brimfield near Ludlow.

The Battalion H.Q. moved around the area frequently. In March 1941, after only 3 months, it had moved to Spilsby, later to Chapel St. Leonards, Grimsthorpe Castle and finally to Tattershall. By January 1942, after a fairly uneventful 18 months and with the threat of a German invasion over, the 6th Bn. were taken off coastal duties, with little to do the men soon grew restless. The Officers came up with the idea of a long distance march in an attempt to break the existing record. Initially a platoon of 17 men was formed from volunteers of Y Coy. led by 2/Lt. M.J.A. (Moss) Walters. However the spirit of competition spread and soon a platoon from each company was entered. Leaving Tattershall on different days and marching by the same route to the Depot in Shrewsbury some 150 mile distance. The Battalion. was kept informed in Regimental Orders on a daily basis, and an account is included

During this time moves were afoot that were to change the destiny of the 6th Bn. As the threat of a German invasion receded, and plans for the Liberation of Europe were being hatched, the call for more Artillery Regiments went out.

Chapter Three

THE SHREWSBURY MARCHES
JANUARY - FEBRUARY 1942

At the beginning of the January 1942 the 6th Bn. found itself in the Coningsby area, having been taken off coastal duties in preparation for conversion to a Royal Artillery Regiment.

After their activities along the the North - East coast, the men became restless with the lack of duties. Some of the Officers had the idea of a record breaking attempt on the long distance marching record. A platoon of volunteers from each company would set out from the company area for a march in the quickest time to the Depot in Shrewsbury, a distance of some 150 -160 miles.

And so it was on 28th January 1942, that 17 men from Y Coy, commanded by 2/Lt. MJA (Moss) Walters set out from Company Headquarters in Woodhall Spa. The men were in battle order carrying six days' rations, and they covered 31 miles on their first day. The following day a platoon from X Coy, under the command of 2/Lt. NW Prutton, left their Company Headquarters, this time travelling light with two days rations, and plans to pick up a further four days' rations on the march. They covered 25 miles on their first day. By this time Y Company platoon had covered some 54 miles reaching Radciff-on-Trent, though they were now battling fierce weather conditions.

By the 30th January Y Company Platoon had reached Derby, and in spite of the bad weather conditions had covered some 75 miles. Cases of sore feet were now being reported but the platoon was still intact. On the same day X Company Platoon had reached Bingham, Notts. and managed to secure a further four days' rations, having suffered one casualty from fever.

On the 31st, their 4th day on the road, Y Company Platoon were going strong and had reached Kingston Staffs, some 100 miles distant. X Company Platoon had reached Sudbury, in Derbyshire.

The following day Y Company Platoon were only 14 miles from Shrewsbury when they bedded down for the night at Newport Salop, and early the next morning, on 2nd February, 2/Lt Walters and the men of Y Company Platoon reached the depot, having covered a distance of 154 miles in 5 days and 12 hours, with no casualties. The following day, 2/Lt. Prutton with X Company Platoon also reached the depot in the slightly shorter time of 5 days, 10 hours, having lost two men.

By 9th February, with the progress of the march being posted daily in Regimental Orders, the whole Battalion had been gripped by marching fever, and men were volunteering in dozens in an attempt to beat the record set by X Company Platoon

Not to be outdone a platoon of volunteers from Z company Platoon led by 2/Lt. VR Evans, travelling in light order with two days rations set out on 9th February, covering 30 miles in good weather on their first day. The day after, a fourth platoon from W coy., was raised and set out on their attempt, led by 2/Lt. J. Curtiss. They covered 31 miles on their first day. By this time Z company Platoon had made good progress covering 56 miles in two days and reaching Nottingham.

On 12th Feb. Z company Platoon had reached Lichfield, Staffs., and W Company

Platoon, Sudbury, neither platoon reporting any casualties. The following day Z Company Platoon arrived at the Depot in a new record time of just over 4 days, knocking a day off the previous record. On 14th Feb. W Company Platoon arrived, but failed to improve on the time set by Z Company Platoon the day before.

Having had the advantage of seeing the times set by the previous platoons and their tactics and routes taken, 2/Lt's John Meredith and Len Sturley felt they could do better. So a fifth platoon was raised from a body of volunteers to form a composite H.Q. Platoon. Not so well practised in marching as the former company platoons, the men from HQ. decided it wise to put in a couple of practice marches, one of these included a night march.

On 17th February led by their two Officers and CSM. Bennett the composite platoon from HQ. set out at 8.30 in the morning, determined to beat the impressive feat set by Z Company Platoon, and with good weather on their side, they covered an almighty 40 miles on the first day! By the second day the men had reached Derby, a distance of some 75 miles and on 20th Feb. having marched all through the night, HQ. Company Platoon arrived at the Depot, in a new impressive record time of 3 days 12 hours, knocking a massive 2 days off the first march by Y Company Platoon at the end of January. The distance covered was some 154 miles from HQ in Mareham-Le-Fen. This time could have been improved on still further but for some confusion at breakfast on the second day which cost the platoon an hour.

During the Marches all the platoons were helped by the YMCA, local villagers, and the Police, who had all entered into the spirit of things, and supplied food and plenty of hot tea along the way. Sleeping arrangements were made in village and church halls, in towns and villages en route.

Chapter Four

THE CONVERSION 1ST MARCH 1942
TO 181ST FIELD REGT. RA.

The first mention of the conversion in the War Diary comes not as a grand announcement but in an obscure entry dated 8th January 1942; 'C/O and 4 OR's proceed to Northern Ireland in connection with the conversion to Field regiment RA.'

Bill Busby told me that he was informed of the change as early as november 1941. Not for him the Royal Artillery! Having been in the Infantry since a boy soldier, he accepted a post along with several other Captains and spent his war on the North - West Frontier with the Ghurkas. The rumour of change had already spread amongst the men by that time, and the pride of the 6th Bn., and what the men had become of themselves, and their comradeship was obvious, as I learned from its ex-members. There was huge disappointment in the ranks, who considered themselves as Infantrymen and part of a great Infantry Regiment with a long standing tradition. They need not have feared as events in the following 18 months were to prove that these men were to become as equally efficient with their Field Guns as they were with their rifles, distinguishing themselves in the major battles of North - West Europe as part of a spearhead Division.

A visit by the Commander Royal Artillery (CRA) Northern Command, Brigadier Wainwright, on the 14th February 1942 saw the start of events that were to shape the infant Field Regiment. On the 26th of the same month a recce. party journeyed North to Sedgefield in Yorkshire to find suitable training grounds. These were subsequently rejected. On the 27th February a second sight was recc'd by 2/Lt. ADG Shaw and the new Regiment's first C/O Lt.Col. EO Herbert DSO who assumed command only the day before. This time they journeyed south, to confirm that the new training ground was to be in the Melton Mowbray Area of Leicestershire. The following day the last day of February 1942, the 6th Bn. KSLI which had come together under the oaks of Sherwood Forest in the Summer of 1940 ceased to exist. On the same day, following a war office exam, 484 other ranks of the old 6th Bn. KSLI were re-posted to 181 Field Regiment RA. About 140 men were re-posted to other Battalions of the KSLI and the Herefordshire Regt., and a similar number went to the Pioneer Corps. Regret was expressed at losing these men, but it was pointed out that Artillery had become quite specialised. The Officers of the Battalion were all offered the choice of transferring or being re-posted back to the Infantry. Of these, eighteen Officers decided that after 18 uneventful months on Coastal duty, the chance of a fresh challenge and some action was too much of a temptation and elected to be transferred. A similar number, nineteen, decided that they were going to remain with the Infantry *(see Appendix 10)*. Of the original eighteen who elected to transfer, due to various postings only nine were still with the Regiment when it embarked for France, and by the time the war in Europe was over only five were still with the 181st. For the purpose of moving, the men were organised into Regimental HQ. and three packets, grouped as Gunners, Drivers, and Specialists. At 1020 hrs on the 3rd March 1942 the main body of men left by train from Coningsby station, by now keen on their new adventure and pleased to be leaving the flat fenlands of Lincolnshire. At 1620 the train arrived at Melton

Mowbray station and discharged its cargo of Gunners. RHQ was to disembark at John O'Gaunt station. The Motor Transport left the square at Tattershall at 1215 under command of Capt. Maurice, and arrived without incident. The men who were to be re-posted to the Infantry were left behind to clean up the billets in Coningsby under the direction of Major Askwith. A whole new military language had to be learned by the new Gunners, and a training pamphlet was issued to help them, Privates became Gunners, L/Cpl's - L/Bdr's, Cpl's - Bdr's, and it quickly became apparent that equipment and insignia was in very short supply. The KSLI cap badge was replaced by a mixture of the artillery 'Gun' Badge and 'Grenade' badge. The ex - KSLI personnel were allowed the privilege of retaining their Green FS caps while new arrivals had to wear the Artillery Scarlet and Blue FS cap. Artillery shoulder titles had not arrived, and on the 27th March 1942 after a three week wait, an order was issued as follows:- *The sign, THE KINGS SHROPSHIRE L.I. will be cut down either side of the word SHROPSHIRE. at right angles to the bottom, NO ROUNDED CORNERS.* These shoulder titles were still being worn in August! This mixture of insignia must have presented a strange sight, and it certainly did not please the eyes of a couple of Military Policemen who detained L/Bdr. Fred Parsons on New Street Station whilst returning from leave, the MP's were unconvinced by Fred's explanation and it was a couple of hours and many 'phone calls later before he was allowed to proceed. The ex - Infantry Officers were allowed the privilege of retaining their Infantry Green lanyards and KSLI buttons on their Service Dress tunics. The shortage was evident in equipment also, and it was the 10th.March before the first field guns arrived - two of them! A month later they still had only four. There wasn't even any red and blue paint to mark the vehicles. One of the immediate tasks was to bring the Regiment up to strength, This was to be done by the posting in of RA. Personnel who started arriving almost immediately. During these early days Dudley Shaw remained the C/O's 'right hand man' and received instructions that no officers or NCO's should unpack before being interviewed, and many never got to unpack at all! It was by selecting only the very best men, which built the foundations of this fine Regiment to-be. By the 10th March over 30 officers and NCO's had joined. This was to continue throughout the month and afterwards, and would include Gunners, Signallers, Storemen, and Drivers, who would help the ex - Infantry men become Gunners. On the 29th March a national day of prayer was held. This parade was vividly recalled by one of the ex-KSLI officers, Lt. Philip Mulholland, not for its piety but for the unforeseen consequences of marching Royal Artillery and Light Infantry men together. Place of honour at the head was given to the Royal Artillery, who were quickly caught up and almost overtaken by the ex-Light Infantry men with their quick marching pace! Which caused much hair pulling by the BSM's.

Chapter Five

ARTILLERY TRAINING, AND A MOVE NORTH
MARCH 1942 - APRIL 1944

It is obvious from the War Diary that training began in earnest and with great gusto. order and counter - order dogged the early days, but it wasn't long before army structure established a programme. The ex-KSLI Officers were posted to Artillery training school for a crash course, the Captains to Larkhill, Salisbury Plain, and the Subalterns to Catterick. These Officers were posted back to the Regiment (officially) on the 1st August 1942 although the Regimental War Diary records them as returning on the 1st of September! I have not been able to confirm why exactly, and none of my Officers can remember! Meanwhile back in Melton Mowbray, the infant Regiment under the guidance of its new Artillery personnel, many of whom wore the riband of the North Africa campaign, began its retraining. There was much hard work ahead and little time to do it in. Initially the Regiment was parcelled into three Batteries which was the normal war establishment procedure, these were designated 'Q' Bty. which would train the the drivers, R Bty. the largest, would train the Gunners, and finally S Bty. which would train the Signallers and specialists (redesignated 11/3/42 Q:R:P) After the Gunners this was the most important section and always the one most difficult to keep up to strength. Out of a total strength of about 600 men 120 were Signallers, and due to wastage and shortage 160 fully trained men were always needed, being the most technical section. Finding men with the right aptitude was a constant problem and many came from the Royal Artillery. Each Battery, consisted of three Troops. After a couple of months, one Troop from each training Battery would be re-posted, to form three permanent Batteries. Thus each eventual Battery would be a complete unit, each having its own complement of Drivers, Gunners and Signaller/Specialists. This, coupled with the fact that more than half of the Regiment had served together as Infantrymen for 18 months, no doubt moving between companies, meant that the men knew each other very well, it was this which forged a bond of comradeship recalled by all of the ex-members that I have interviewed, including the Officers, who took the care of their men very seriously, whilst of course maintaining discipline. This was recognised by the men, who, in turn had enormous respect for their Officers. Only one of the Officers was never taken to heart by the men owing to his lack of compassion. And his mettle was tested in battle, when one of my interviewees, (Dvr) Charlie Spence from Scotland told me that whilst training this Officer talked at length, of thrashing the Hun, only to discover when the testing time came, that he didn't have the stomach for it himself. He left Regiment at the end of 1944 for a War Office job. Shortly after this reorganisation the new Regiment moved North to the moorlands of West Yorkshire to the areas, Newbiggin, Otterburn and Friskney to perfect their shooting skills.

Chapter Six

THE 15TH SCOTTISH DIVISION

The 7th November 1942 saw a visit to the Regiment by the GOC. of the 15th Scottish Division, Maj.Gen. GHA. McMillan, without pomp or ceremony. This is how the Regimental war diary announced the Order of Battle for the 181st field Regiment RA. They were to become the only English Artillery Regiment of the re-formed 15th Scottish Division, the other two being the 131st and the 190th, Field Regiments. The only other 'Sassenachs' were the Machine Gun Bn. -The 1st Bn. Middlesex Regiment. The 15th Scottish Division was formed on the 2nd September 1939, from the 52nd Lowland Division, an untried mixed Infantry Division from the Highland and Lowland Regiments of Scotland, that would have to maintain, and live up to the proud tradition that was earned by its predecessor, which fought with pride and honour and distinguished itself in the Great War of 1914 - 18. The Divisional sign would be the letter 'O' in white, it being the fifteenth of the alphabet, as worn by it's predecessors, however the red triangular 'Scotch' within the circle was dispensed with. For twelve Months the letter 'O' would remain empty, until permission was granted, after a visit by his Majesty the King on 31st October 1940, for the Rampant Lion of Scotland to appear within the circle, this would be red against a gold background all set on a black 'patch' and worn with pride on each upper sleeve below the Regimental title, by every man in the Division. Each Artillery Regiment in the Division would support one of the three Divisional Infantry Brigades: the 44th (Lowland) Bde; the 46th (Highland) Bde; and the 227th (Highland) Bde.. Each Brigade contained three Infantry Battalions . The 181st now moved further north to begin training with its own Brigade, the 44th Lowland. This comprised of three Battalions, the 8th Bn. Royal Scots (RS); the 6th Bn. Royal Scots Fusiliers (RSF); and the 6th Bn. King's Own Scottish Borderers (KOSB). Each Field Battery was assigned to its own Infantry Battalion that it would support in battle 'Q' Bty. would support 8th RS.; R Bty. - 6th KOSB.; P Bty.- 6th RSF. The Batteries were to be finally redesignated and numbered 177; 178; 179; on 1st January 1943.

THE ARTILLERY FIELD REGIMENT

An Artillery Field Regiment was a mobile unit of 3:45" - 18/25 pounder Howitzer Guns, but better known as 25 - pounders. 24 guns in total plus vehicles and workshops and had an establishment of 672 all ranks. Attached to the Regiment was a Signal Section from the Royal Corps of Signals, and a Light Aid Detachment (L.A.D.) from the Royal Army Ordnance Corps to maintain guns and vehicles*. The Regiment was divided into three Batteries, each with eight guns, and a Battery was divided into two Troops of 4 guns each, plus a Battery HQ. and two Troop HQ's. There was 204 officers and men in each Battery, the Battery was commanded by a Major. The Troop was commanded by a Captain and had a 'left' and 'right' section, each with two guns. Each section was divided into two subsections of one gun each commanded by a Sergeant, known as 'number one'. there were six men operating the gun; A Layer, who had the responsibility of bringing the gun on target, following instructions from the gun Sergeant via the Command Post. The gun had to be re-laid after every shell fired. According to procedure each 'lay' had to be checked by the Gun Sergeant, invariably, in the urgency of battle this was overlooked. The layer bore great responsibility, one or two degrees out could result in shells over shooting the target and alerting the enemy to the imminent attack. However, far worse was 'short shooting' which resulted in shells landing amongst his own infantry, 'friendly fire' in modern parlance, this was the Gunners' worst nightmare and the one he feared most. The rest of the crew consisted; two loaders, who fed shells into the breech as fast as the gun could be laid and fired, and three ammunition men, who selected shot, which could be HE (high explosive), airburst, AP (armour piercing), smoke etc. and set charges and fuse timings for impact and distance. Orders were given by the Gun Sergeant, via the command post, who received orders from the Forward Observation Post, which could be anywhere up to a mile in front of of the guns with the forward line of Infantry. Manned by the Troop commander, his Signaller, and his Bdr/ Ack, whose job was to plot the range of the shell. This was done with a set formula based on trigonometry, taking into consideration, air pressure, wind direction / speed, lie of the land etc.The FOP could be any building, a bren-carrier, a tank or even a dug-out anywhere enemy movement could be observed, these prominent buildings or features would, themselves, be pinpointed by enemy guns making them a very dangerous place to be. This team would calculate distances and direction, and choose targets for bombardment, these would be signalled back via Battalion HQ, to Battery HQ, and finally to Troop Command Post, and to the Gun Sergeant. Being so far in front, the observation post team hardly saw anything of their own guns, but had the satisfaction of seeing the results when they spoke. With the exception of one or two, most of the FOO's (forward observation officers) were ex-KSLI Officers, infantrymen, who knew instinctively what was required by the footsoldier. The ideal range was about 3,000 yds, but the gun was accurate for about 11,000 yds in good conditions.

* The Royal Electrical and Mechanical Engineers was formed in 1942 from the Engineering Branch of The Royal Army Ordnance Corps and subsequently operated L.A.D workshops.

Chapter Seven

TRAINING WITH THE DIVISION 1943/44

The move north brought the 181st under Northern Command, prior to joining the 15th (S)Div. in July 1943. The men were issued with the appropriate badge, this was a green apple on a blue diamond shaped badge worn on the upper sleeve. Throughout 1942 the intensive training continued. Regular bulletins were issued which kept the men in touch with their progress, highlighting any areas that needed attention. Brigade and Divisional exercises were carried out on an almost weekly basis, going under such headings as, *Celerity: Spartan: Salop: Jorrocks: Gallop: Bovril: Macdove: Tinker: Olympus: Punchbowl: Clansmen: Eno: Eagle: Blackcock:*

On 1st January 1943 the Batteries were finally redesignated : 177: 178 :179., and in the same month the Regiment was stationed at Long Framlington and Ross Links, however exercises would take them to all parts of the Yorkshire moors; two further quick moves found the RHQ. at Haydon Bridge in April 1943, and in June, the whole Regiment was photographed in their Battery areas, with individual photo's taken of the Troops and their Officers, many of which survive today, as mementoes for their proud ex-members. Later, in the same month they were at Wykeham Abbey. All guns of the Regiment had been zeroed and calibrated to fire in co-ordination at a given target on the 19th and 20th Feb 1943.

In September 1943 came the news that the 15th Scottish Division was to become part of 8 Corps, it being the only mixed infantry division, the other two being Armoured Divisions. This would entail further training with the tanks of the the 6th Guards Tank Bde. although replaced by 227 Infty Bde before D-Day, they were to meet again on the battle field were they fought side by side. Thus all the elements worked together; Armour, Artillery, and Infantry in an effective and co-ordinated manner. For this the Regiment moved with 8 Corps, to the area, Boroughbridge, and Ripon, in Yorkshire, where RHQ was at Hildebrand Barracks in Harrogate. Altogether this training was designed to produce a feeling of trust and mutual respect that would be taken to the battlefield, to make the 15th Scottish Division, a hard hitting, spearhead Division that fought from the break-out of Normandy through France, Belgium, Holland, across the Siegfried Line, through the Reichswald Forest into the heart of Germany, and the shores of the Baltic.

As 1944 approached the training became ever more critical, firing practice continued on a daily basis at the ranges in Buckton, Baysdale, and Osmotherly, so too did the Inter-Brigade, and Divisional exercises, On the 23rd March 1944 the Division was honoured by a visit from H.M.The King and shortly afterwards by the Prime Minister Winston Churchill on the 31st March. Rumours were strong in the Regiment that their destination was to be India, so strong indeed that Gnr. Percy Lewis had his head shaved in preparation for the heat. But he need not have bothered, for it was to be France, as part of the Europe Liberation force.

The primary task of a Field Artillery unit is to provide fire support which will enable the Infantry to reach its objective. This is achieved by the guns laying down a 'Rolling Barrage' - a line of exploding shells that moves along just in front of the first line of Infantry. Too far in front and the support is lost, as the enemy are alerted, too close and there is great danger that a shell falling short will land amongst the men. In addition, concentrations of fire can be bought down on specific targets, enemy strongholds, armoured concentrations, enemy Artillery positions and the like. The three Batteries may be called on to bring down a barrage on one particular target this was known as a *'Mike'* and on a wider scope the Divisional Commander Royal Artillery may call upon all three Artillery Regiments in the Division to *hammer* a specific target this was known as an *'Uncle'* This is what the training was geared to achieve, a bond and a feeling of mutual trust between the Gunners and the Infantry, to instill in the Gunner that he must never let the footsoldier down! In addition to all this the 25 - pounder was designed so that it could be used as an effective anti tank gun, when the layer would fire over *open sights*. A great deal of time and effort was put into this training, and indeed during the battle for Normandy the Regiment received orders to *'prepare to fire over open sights, range 500 - 1000 yds'*. The German tanks were thought to be on the point of breaking through the line.

A new Commanding Officer arrived with the Division, Lt.Col. A.C.E. Devereux RA to succeed Lt.Col. E.O. Herbert DSO, and also a new CRA (Commander Royal Artillery) Brig. R. Hilton MC DFC to replace Brig. A.A. Middleton of Northern Command. Brig. Hilton, nicknamed 'Bosun' was a Royal Artillery Officer who was awarded a Distinguished Flying Cross for bravery, having joined the newly formed Royal Flying Corps during the Great War, but switched allegiance to become a fine Artillery Officer with new ideas on how a Field Artillery unit should operate. Lessons having been learnt in the desert campaign of North Africa. Major Dudley Shaw credits the huge success of the Divisional Artillery to these two men. First and foremost was the men's fitness, and many of the men recall the tough programme of cross-country route marches, and physical training. This was to encourage determination and stamina, and also team work! All types of sport were catered for. Boxing, football, cricket, etc. The men competed for prizes, for the best shot, the best kept vehicle, the cleanest gun etc. All designed to encouraged team spirit and pride. Underlining all this was his idea that a Field Artillery should be *mobile*; on the move quickly, moving position, to bring the guns as close as possible to the target for increased accuracy, dispensing with the old idea of always digging gun pits. Instead the gun crew were trained to practice firing off the gun platform, this was a huge iron 'wheel' which, gave the gun a 360 degree arc of fire coupled with the ability to fire from horizontal to almost 90 degrees, and a gun crew that could fire almost twenty rounds per minute in an emergency, made it a devastating and often decisive weapon. So effective, that when used as Divisional Artillery in Normandy. the Germans were convinced it was a new automatic gun.

Chapter Eight

DESTINATION FRANCE
JUNE 1944

On 22nd April 1944 the Regimental War Diary records: *'Regiment moves to new area'* This area was Worthing in Sussex, which by this time had become one huge army camp, as the concentration area for the Allied Invasion Force. The H.Q. for the 15th Scottish Division was Knepp Castle, near West Grinstead, and the three Artillery Regiments were stationed between Ashington, Worthington and Lancing. During this time the men were encouraged to take part in the recreation provided to prevent boredom and to keep them fit. This included inter-Regimental football matches, boxing tournaments athletics and greyhound race meetings which were held at Brighton Football Stadium. On the morning of 6th June 1944 the men watched in awe as suddenly, without warning, the sky began to fill with wave upon wave of allied aircraft all heading in one direction, France. The invasion of German occupied Europe had begun. A couple of nights later at midnight, the Regiment was moved close to Tilbury Docks and billeted in a barbed wire compound. The vehicles, with their engines all water-proofed, and guns were parked for easy removal, and some of the men were allowed passes for a last night out on the town. The following day their money was changed into Francs and the men were issued with life-belts and *'bags vomit'*. On 10th June the Regiment was on its way to the Docks. Gnr Charlie Spence remembers it well. *"It was a wonderful journey, the streets were heaving with cheering crowds, and the housewives were passing up sandwiches, for the crossing. and the men handing us bottles of beer"* It was a marvellous feeling for him to be part of it all. They were due to start loading on the Sunday but, incredulously, as Lt John Thomlinson recalled the Dockers refused to work on their Sunday off! Eventually the Regiments, vehicles, guns and everything else that made up an Artillery Field Regiment was loaded aboard two Liberty Ships. Capt Tommy Stokes recalls that 177 Bty. was aboard the *Fort Biloxi*.

Once aboard the men made themselves as comfortable as possible and were issued with rations. Among these was a variety of canned foods which came supplied with its own internal wick. This was lit and within a few minutes produced a tin of hot food that could be eaten straight away! A wonderful innovation that, strangely, was never seen again. Events moved quickly now, all the time the men eager to get news of how 'our lads' were faring on the beaches and just as eager to get 'stuck in'. On the evening of 12th June, D-Day plus 6, the Fort Biloxi slipped its moorings and began its journey into history. The following day, 13th June the remainder of the Regiment was also under way, and on that evening both ships were anchored off Southend to await their convoy. It was 14th June before the convoy came together and started on its way at 2100 hrs. The men occupied themselves playing cards, and many put to good use their 'bags vomit' Although the crossing was indeed fairly smooth, (a situation that was to change dramatically), and met no opposition. By 2200 hrs on 15th June the convoy was anchored off Arromanches The most vivid recollections was the fantastic sight of so many ships as 'far as one could see' and the night-time fireworks display from every gun available, aimed at any enemy plane that dared to come within striking distance. Some of the Artillery

Greyhounds were a feature of 6 KSLI the men were encouraged to race their own.
On the left is C/O RBS Munn.

Capt. Bristowe and Lt. Prutton with NCO's of X Coy. 6 KSLI.

I

Officers of 6 KSLI, L/R 2/Lt. Spooner, Capt. Rev. Hughes,
C/O. Lt.Col. RBS Munn, RSM. Brown, 2/LT. Paddock.

Intelligence Section 6 KSLI with O/C 2/Lt ADG Shaw.

No. 4 Mortar detachment, Rear: Pte's Blount, Richards, Unknown,
Front: Pte's Jamieson, Whent, Hooton.

L/Cpl. Adams, Sgt. Neale, 2Lt. Meredith, Sgt. Tunnicliffe, L/Cpl. Bowden, L/Cpl. Sheperd.
Note the pre-1939 old style uniform worn by Sgt. Neale.

6 KSLI Cadre Platoon Wellbeck Abbey 1940, Rear: L/Cpl Burgess, Pts Cox Catchpole,
Morris, Caler McCoy, Hartshill, Morris, Sgt Meredith. Middle: L/Cpls Polley, Whittaker,
Walters, Causer, Sgt's Mills, Walker, Bennett, L/Cpl Bowhill. Front: L/Cpls Brookes, Davis,
Davies, Hill, Pte Wheeler, L/Cpl Fisher.

Capt. (Adjutant) Ted Corbett 6 KSLI.

Lt. Johnny Gibbons with a Section from 6 KSLI.

Final Officers Mess 6 KSLI 1942. Rear: 2/Lt's Jacques, Hyde, Sturley, U/K, U/K, Capt Grischotti, U/K, U/K, U/K, 2/Lts Macowen, Matthewman, Shields, Paddock, Meredith, Haydon, U/K. Front: 2/Lt Raitz, Capt Corbett, Capt Maurice, Lt. Col. RBS Munn MC, Capt Martin, Capt Bristowe, 2/Lt Hyne.

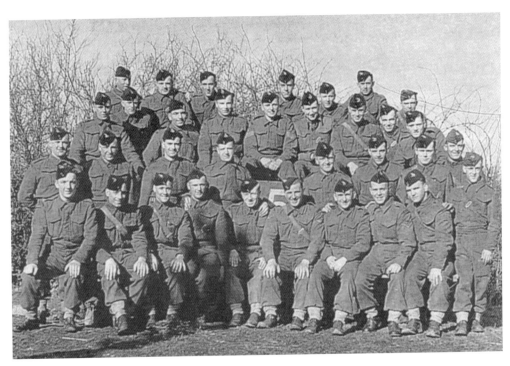

Composite HQ Coy Platoon - winners of the Shrewsbury March, Jan/Feb 1942.

Sgt. Dick Fletcher, Sgt. George Gibbons, Bdr. Mottram. All members of C Troop.

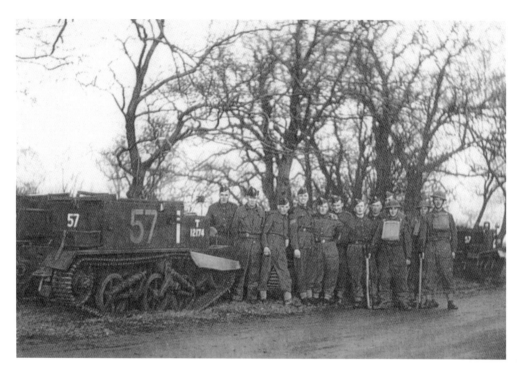

Bren-Carrier Platoon 6 KSLI, Dec 1941.

Bren Carrier Platoon 6 KSLI. Rear: Sgt Bourne, Cpl Powell, L/Cpl Eden, U/K, U/K, U/K U/K
Middle: Pte Wakely, L/Cpl Ashton, U/K, Pte Whittle, Cpl Mullan,
Front: U/K, L/Cpl George, Pte Fowler, U/K.

181 team/44 Bde. Endurance Competition, 20th November 1943.

Troop Commanders 181 Field Regiment, with a mixture of S.D. caps and Balmorals.
Capts: Owen, Buchanan, Meredith and Clements.

C Troop Signallers, L/R: Bdr Fairhurst, Gnrs Edwards,
Whittington, Braithwaite, Capt Meredith.

RA Training Course, Catterick, April 1942
2nd Lts:J. Meredith, K A Hyne, J R Jacques, L Sturley.

Officers 178 Bty, Rear: 2/Lt McLeod, Lt. Clements, Lt Buchanan, Lt Jones, 2/Lt Todd.
Front: Capt Meredith, Capt Martin, Maj Moorshead, Capt Shaw, Lt Trewby.

Officers 179 Bty, Rear: Lt Mulholland, Lt Jones, Lt Hewitt, Lt Murray, Lt Boyd, Lt Porter
Front: Capt Prutton, Capt Bristow, Maj Sedgwick, Capt Attewell.

C Troop, June 1944. Rear: Bdr Hall, Bdr Forknall, Bdr Edwards, U/K, Balcombe, U/K, Willey, Sig Smith 63, Lewis, U/K, Adams, Smith 88. Row 3: Gnr Neal, Dvr McInery, Fox, Basnett, U/K, Dvr Compton, U/K, Ball, Scott, May, U/K, U/K, Bryant, Smith. Row 2: Evans 33, Parsons, Dvr Cotton, Barnes, Sig Abbiss, U/K, Sig Whittingham, Sig Broomhall, Sig Adams, U/K, Sig Huyton, Sig Woods, Edwards, Sig Briathwaite, Hassle, Bdr Furlough. Front: Bdr Dalton, Bdr Kilby, Sgt Mottram, Sgt Darby, BSM Cook, Lt Clements, Capt Meredith, 2/Lt Todd, Sgt Gunn, Sgt Powell, Sgt Packer, Bdr Aspley, L/Sgt Eden.

HQ 181 Field Regt. RA, Ridley Hall, June 1944. Rgtl HQ. June 1944, Rear: U/K, U/K, U/K, Bty Clerk, U/K, U/K Bdr Cook, U/K, U/K, U/K, U/K, Sig Jones, U/K, Bdr Bennet, Dvr King, Dvr Kendrew, Evans, Dvr Snooks, Devaney. Row 3: U/K, U/K, Dvr Spence, Sig Garvey, U/K, U/K, Sig Billingham, U/K, U/K, Bdr Evans, L/Bdr Ashton, Dvr Tapperal, U/K, U/K, Jones, Evans. Row 2: U/K Sig, U/K Dvr, Sig Chamberlain, U/K, Dvr Garland, U/K, Dvr Hall, U/K, Sig Symes, Brown, Clewes, Forrest, Dvr Clerk. Front: Pye, Bdr George, Lucas, U/K, U/K Cook, Dvr Ingeson, BQMS Norcross, Capt Trewby, Lt Mcloed, BSM Norton, Sgt Hunt, Bdr Marsden, Snape, Owen.

XII

D Troop Ridley Hall June 1944, Rear: U/K, U/K, U/K, Watson, Bennall, Mills. Row 3: Hartshorne, U/K, Prince, Jones, U/K, U/K, Wall, U/K, U/K, Fisher, Fellows, Daffern, U/K, U/K, U/K, Gwatkin. Row 2: Parsons, Kirk, Poutney, Clarke, U/K, U/K, U/K, Tudor, U/K, U/K, U/K, Beardsmore, Cuff, U/K, U/K. Front Row: Drake, Jinks, Hyde, U/K, Sgt Foster, Sgt Guy, Sgt Leighton, Lt Jones, Capt Shaw, Lt Buchanan, BSM Oliver, Sgt Layton, Sgt Holdsworth, Bdr Clark, Bdr Griffiths.
Seated: Lacey, Turvey, Maddox, Morriss, Evans, Williams.

B Troop 177 Bty 2nd June 1944. Back Row: Gnrs Pugh, Bramald, Daltry, Godfrey, Bowell, Baker, Goy, Todd, Andrews, Gordon, L/Bdr Moyle. Row 4: Gnrs Coley, Geeson, Hughes, Dimmock, Stevens, Cummings, Hamilton, Pardoe, Husband, Jones, Bates. Row 3 Gnrs Cartwright, Gregory, Houlgrave, Punton, Clapham, Roberts, Brook. Pick, Berrick, Fitzmaurice, James 70, Lewis, Douglas, Kelso. Row 2: Bdrs Saddler, Hopper, Luke, Sgts Fletcher, Bull, BSM Clacker, Lt McOwen, Capt Cory-Wright, Lt Stokes, Sgts Desborough, Winter, Sturley, Clee, Bdrs Bugler, Crouch. Front Row: Gnrs Pendlebury, Marlow, Griffiths, McDonald, Tighe, Jennings, James 96, Kinsey, Wood. Absent: Stokoe, Neville, Laycock.

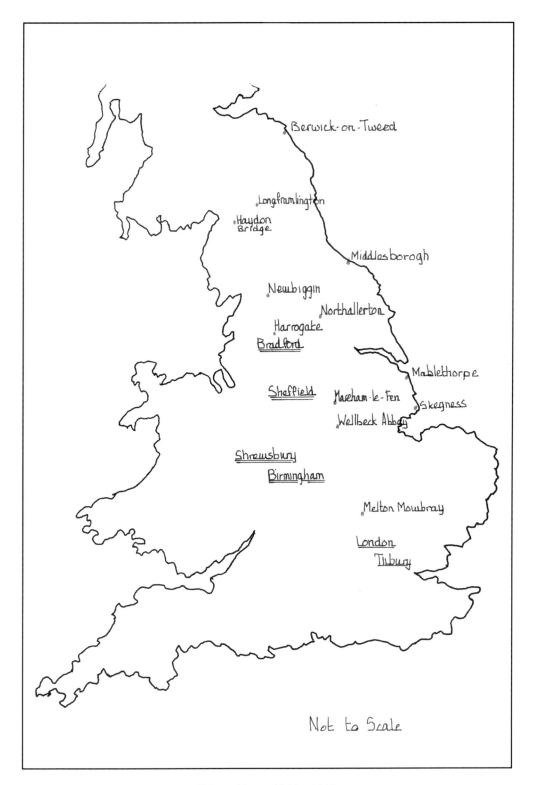

Berwick-on-Tweed

Longframlington

Haydon
Bridge

Middlesborogh

Newbiggin

Northallerton

Harrogate
Bradford

Mablethorpe

Sheffield   Mareham-le-Fen
Skegness

Wellbeck Abbey

Shrewsbury
Birmingham

Melton Mowbray

London
Tilbury

Not to Scale

HQ positions. 1940 - 1942.

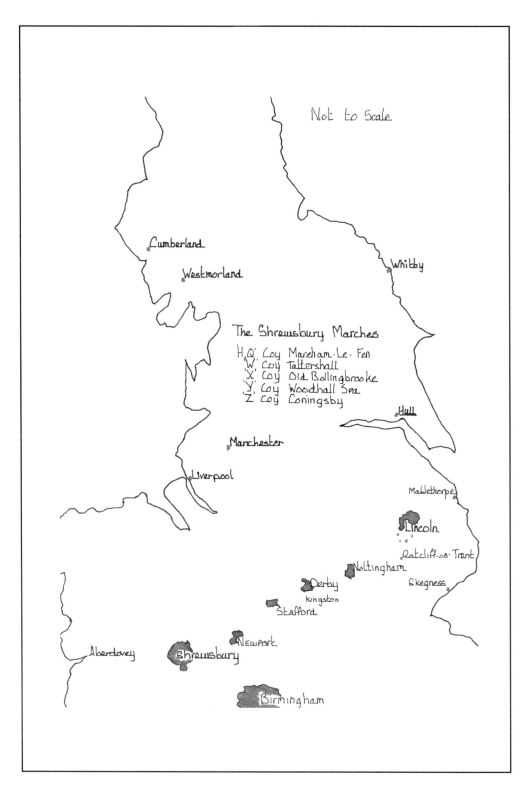

Not to Scale

Cumberland

Westmorland

Whitby

The Shrewsbury Marches
H.Q. Coy   Mareham-Le-Fen
'W' Coy   Tattershall
'X' Coy   Old Bollingbrooke
'Y' Coy   Woodhall Spa
'Z' Coy   Coningsby

Manchester

Liverpool

Hull

Mablethorpe

Lincoln

Ratcliff-on-Trent

Nottingham

Skegness

Derby

Kingston

Stafford

Aberdovey

Newport

Shrewsbury

Birmingham

Route covered by the Shrewsbury Marches, Jan/Feb 1942.

XVI

personnel were ordered to man the ship's guns, others took cover beneath vehicles and below decks as there was a danger from falling shrapnel. The unloading of vehicles and guns began almost immediately with the first Troops scrambling down the nets slung over the the sides of the ship and dropping into the L.C.l.'s (Landing Craft Infantry). This was a tricky manoeuvre in anything but the most calm of waters, with the LCI rising and falling with the swell, and a man probably carrying upwards of 60 pounds on his back had to ensure his timing was spot on! His chances of surviving a drop into the ocean were almost nil, Many men witnessed one poor chap having his legs crushed between the two craft, and several dropping into the sea. Charlie Spence recalls the moment he went overboard. *"The sea was getting rougher and rougher and the Landing Craft just couldn't get close enough; We had seen one chap get crushed between the two Craft, I suggested to my pal Ralph McMorland that we should jump inside my vehicle as the Drivers were to watch for their own vehicle going over and to follow. Jumping into the cab seemed a lot safer, against regulation of course"*. Gnr John May also remembers several men going over perched on top of the vehicles. Charlie's Landing Craft took them so far up the beach that his lorry didn't even get wet tyres. No such luck for everyone, many men were dropped chest deep into the sea with a full pack on. Dudley Shaw remembers going over the side of the ship on a scramble net as a terrifying experience. *"The net had to be pulled away from the side of the ship to enable a grip. Looking down at the craft which was there one second and gone the next was awful, somehow I got it right and landed in the bottom of the landing craft"*. The many hours spent on water-proofing the vehicles paid off handsomely as none suffered from waterlogged engines.

It wasn't long before the situation became impossible and the French coast was about to receive the worst storm in living memory. Most of 178 Bty. and 179 Bty. were unloaded quickly and without too much incident. Capt.Philip Mulholland also recalls reaching the beach without getting his feet wet. All the initial wave landed on Juno beach near the village of Courseulles, and the Regimental Diary records on 19th June; *"One ship emptied RHQ and 177 still to land"* Just prior to the storm a huge L.C.T. (Landing Craft Tank) unable to return to the beach with its load, had been lashed to the side of the ship, Broke loose and was cast adrift. On board were 2 guns several lorries including a half-track, and RHQ, all lost at sea. Although captured briefly by an American Cruiser, it broke loose a second time and was smashed on the rocks. Apart from a single lorry which was recovered by a group of men including Capt. Tommy Stokes all the equipment was lost. The men who remained on the ships had a very rough time of it, and mixed feelings; some of them glad not to be on the beaches, others feeling trapped out at sea at the mercy of the German guns. It was 21st June before the remainder of the Regiment landed, this time further down the coast at St. Come de Fresne. A couple of days later the Regiment came together at Brecy, the Divisional concentration area some 8 miles inland where the forward positions had been recc'd, gun positions prepared and ammo dumped. It was only a few days before the missing equipment was replaced, but time enough for the Officers and men of 177 Bty. to suffer some severe leg pulling for turning up without any guns or lorries! During this period the Regiment suffered what is believed to be its first casualty, Recorded by Capt. Philip Mulholland. Signals Sgt. Bentley (ex-KSLI) ran into the back of a lorry on his motorbike during a night move as the Regiment moved forward, and was reported to be back on his way to Blighty before the first shots were fired.

Chapter Nine

INTO BATTLE AND A BAD START
JUNE 26TH 1944

On 24th June the Regimental War Diary, in one undramatic line, records, *'Regiment moves into action at Bronay'* Here was an unfortunate slip of the Military pen which was perpetuated and recorded by the Diaries of all the units of 44 Brigade. The actual name of the village was Brouay, only one letter difference, but there is no doubt that there was a spelling mistake, probably on the direction boards which was copied and re-copied, and it seems almost offensive to alter it after some 50 odd years, as Bronay is the name recalled by all of the Regiment's old members. Two days later on the 26th June, the 181st Field Regt. was to take part in its first action with the Divisional Artillery. The operation known as *Epsom*, was, for the 15th Scottish Div, "The Battle of the Scottish Corridor" renamed "The Battle of the Odon". Originally to commence on 18th June but postponed because of the shipping hold up. H-Hour was Scheduled for 7:30am. Laying down the barrage were to be 900 guns including those of three cruisers out at sea: 344 were field and medium guns. Try and imagine how these young men felt, many only 18 or 19 years old, who, just a few years earlier had been in civvy street, working on farms, in factories and shops. Their hour had arrived.

The Infantry cursed the drizzly weather, this would mean no air support. At 7:29 orders came over the tannoy to the waiting guns *"stand by to fire serial 1"*, and 1 minute later with an ear-splitting roar several hundred guns began hurling their shells into the enemy. ex-Gunners always tell me that it was strange how they only seemed to hear the first crack of the gun. After that the noise was rather like standing under a bridge with a train going over it! The crew could fire about 12 rounds per minute, more on rapid fire. Each man in the crew hard at his task, the layer crouched over his sights, listening for instructions from his No.1, the loaders hurling 25pd. shells and charges into the breech, and the ammo men lugging 1 cwt. boxes of charges about, and setting fuses, and above the din the No.1 screaming instructions at his layer for sight adjustments, instructions which started perhaps a half mile or so in front at the FOP. This was the moment that the 181st Field Regiment had been training for. Signaller Bill Smith recalled the heat of battle; *"Our 24 guns plus the heavy and medium Batteries, firing one shell every ten or more seconds almost drove us mad, it went on for hours"*. In his book, 'LION RAMPANT' (page 53) Robert Woolcombe (2i/c A coy. 6th Bn. KOSB) describes this first action thus:

'The minute hand touched 7:30... On the second, nine hundred guns of all calibres, topped by the fifteen inch broadsides from the distant battleships lying off the beaches, vomited their inferno. Concealed guns opened from fields, hedges and farms in every direction around us, almost as if arranged in tiers. During short pauses between salvoes more guns could be heard, and right away further guns, filling and reverberating the very atmosphere with a sustained muffled hammering. It was like rolls of thunder, only it never slackened'.

The day before on 25th June disaster had struck 181, before their guns were fired in anger, their position was heavily shelled by the German guns. A-Sub gun took a direct hit and three of its crew were killed, Sgt. Arthur Gunn and Gnr's Stan Wheaton and Ralph McMorland.

Three others were seriously wounded, Bdr. Dalton, and Gnr's Curtiss and May. John 'Ginger' May was only 19 years old at the time, and his right arm was so badly damaged it had to be amputated. I'm pleased to say 'Ginger' is alive and well and living in Kent, and I was pleased to visit him in May '98, after writing to him over a couple of years. An Officer was also seriously wounded, I believe his name was D'Ambruiel, and he lost his feet. All of the casualties are mentioned in the Regimental War Diary though not by name. Entered by hand after the diary had been typed up for the day thus: *1 Officer wounded, 3 OR's killed 3 OR's wounded*.

The area had previously been held by the Canadian Artillery, and afterwards it became known that the position was targeted every day at about the same time. There was some anger that the Regiment hadn't been warned about this. I asked Bill Smith for his memories of the incident, he told me:- *"One other Gunner and I had been detailed to remove some dead animals and also some German dead from in front of the gun site. The job done we were going back to our guns when the shelling began. I was quite near the guns and lay down in a small dip, the rest of the crew were in a slit trench. BSM. Cooke yelled out 'who's that out there', Smith 63 I answered, 'well get in here' The trench was full, but I squeezed in behind Albert Smith. It was a heavy barrage, Albert was sitting on my knees, so squashed up were we. Suddenly, Albert started to tremble violently, and I could tell he lost control of his bowels, after a few seconds my bowels turned to water, and I too had to get changed. I felt afterwards that I would have been better off staying where I was, in the open. However I never got the shakes again. We heard a commotion on the other guns, and went down to learn that the gun my mate John May was on had been hit and some of the crew were dead and others wounded. Among them John, who had his right arm almost severed, as the arm was only hanging by a shred of flesh the Medic removed it. Young McMorland, who had been put on the gun in my place was dead, as was the Sgt soon to be. A sad day, and not to be the last that the Troop would suffer casualties."*

It's almost impossible to imagine their terror, and I often wonder now where my Dad was at the time, and what was he experiencing? I'll never know, but that baptism of fire is etched into every one of my ex-Gunners memories. Sgt Fred Darby, who was my Dads No.1, told me he watched the shell as it lost height to land amongst the men of A-sub. Sgt Gunn, a morbid man as Bill Smith recalls, often told his men that he had a feeling he wouldn't 'make it' and it was reported to me by Bill who was there, that he was found in his gun position, and his last words - *"I told you, I knew it,"* there wasn't a mark on him. These lads were originally buried in the Churchyard at Brouay Church, Charlie Spence remembers it as a very sombre dignified occasion, all of the Battery Officers were on parade, for the salute. The men now lie at rest in the War Cemetery at Brouay. Charlie sent me an original postcard of Brouay Church, marking the boys burial spot with a cross.

Sgt Gunn was a regular soldier, a Gunnery Instructor, who was a last minute choice for the invasion. He was a stickler for doing everything by the book, including being ready at the gun for daily gun drill, probably the reason for the whole crew becoming casualties. My Dad trained with this crew before the invasion, and only left when he was appointed L/Bdr! 'Ginger' May knew Dad very well, and remembered him as quiet and unassuming, steady, and always helpful. A very accurate description.

'Ginger' was evacuated to a Field Dressing Station, where part of his shattered arm was removed by the Medical Officer, Capt. Stuart Lowden, who was killed in a minefield only three months later. Arriving for further surgery in England he ended up at Chapel Allerton hospital,

Leeds, where the Surgeon did him a strange favour by removing more of his arm to above the elbow. Ginger told me that this has been worth 'a few extra bob' to him over the years in pension.

The Battle of Normandy has been well documented and far better accounts written, but it was here that the 15th Scottish Division was to earn itself a fearsome reputation, never faltering, keeping up the tradition earned by it's predecessors in a previous war. here the bond was forged between the Infantry and their Gunners. Again, from his book, Robert Woolcombe pays tribute on page 78 and writes:

"And our own Gunners answered, they were magnificent whether we could have stayed our ground but for our artillery is doubtful, here was forged our bond with them, as attack after attack was mounted the deadly 25pnd gun-howitzers poured out their deluges. The enemy so near that the Gunners were bringing their concentrations almost on top of their own Infantry." And later on page 92 speaking of a weary Forward Observation Officer. *"His face pale and tired, his eyes unhappy, the nerve of this man who time after time must have saved our lives with his guns, and had wrought such havoc."*

On the morning of that first day in battle, at about mid-day the Regiment lost its first and only Officer, Capt AJJ. Cory-Wright, B Troop Commander 177 Bty. He was killed when a shell landed close to his party, whilst moving forward on foot, to recce his forward observation position. Cory-Wright, an Artillery Officer, came to the regiment only five days after the conversion, in March 1942 and for a time was Adjutant before being made up to Troop Commander, he is buried in the Churchyard at Tilly-sur-Seulles. His death is entered in the War Diary by name, and hand written.

The Battle Continues

This was the Battle of Normandy for the 181st Field Regiment. At one point the Gunners were ordered to fire over open sights when there was a threat of enemy tanks breaking through, a fire plan of scale 40 was ordered! The men rose to it, and the threat receded. At another stage, target range was down to a mere 800 yds.

The Division's objective was to capture a crossing over the River Odon, and hold it long enough for the 11th Armoured Division to continue the breakout southward. Driving south, the Scots took each one of the strongly defended villages and towns held by fanatical Troops of the battle hardened German army who had been fighting since 1939. Cheux, St. Mauvieu, Mouen, Gavrus, Bougy, Tourville, Everecy. The Field Artillery moved quickly forward in order to provide the most accurate concentration of fire to support their infantry and destroy enemy Armour and strong points. As they moved forward the Gunners became aware of the devastating effect of their barrage, the countryside littered with burning hulks of enemy tanks and transport, the remains of farm animals and enemy dead mangled together under the hail of metal, no time in the hasty advance for burials of either, as Sappers of the Royal Engineers bulldozed through the carnage, and the small Normandy villages were reduced to rubble. An entry from Sgt Dick Fletcher's personal diary for the 5th July reads, *'Moved to St Mauvieu, everything down to the ground and what a stink dead stock all around us, fired quite a few rounds'*. Despite Allied air superiority the Division was bombed and shelled constantly, the Artillery coming in for special attention. The Division continued to press forward driving a corridor into the enemy defences, regardless at times of its undefended flanks. On the 27th June the bridge over the Odon was captured intact by the 2nd Bn. Argyll and Sutherland Highlanders of 227 Bde. For this they were honoured with the title of "Crossing Sweepers". They were presently joined by the 11th Armoured Division who were to continue the breakout.

Fighting With The Yanks

On the 22nd July the entry in Sgt Fletcher's Diary reads, *'Getting ready to move, and are we pleased, Jerry still shelling and bombing.'* And on the following day, *'What a relief to Balleroy and American sector, like going from hell to heaven, how quiet it is - it don't seem natural.'* And so the Divisional history records on exactly the same day, a secret move to the Caumont sector in support of the American 2nd and 5th Airborne division. Capt Dudley Shaw described it as a *'land of milk and honey, plenty of everything'* indeed it was hard to believe the carnage that was going on just a few miles to the west. This was the first time that the men of the 15th Scottish were fighting alongside the Americans, and our boys were mightily impressed with their equipment and rations, and the generous Americans were only too happy to share everything with their British allies. On the 30th July the attack on Caumont began and the Gunners of 181 were in the the thick of it, as all the Divisional Artillery was called on again to provide support for the Troops in Operation "Bluecoat" Once again the Divisions task would be to drive another hole in the enemy defences at Caumont and to establish itself on point 309, Quarry Hill, in order to protect the right flank of 30 corps, and to open the way for the British armour. The attack began on the 30th July. Sgt Fletcher's Diary gives us a day by day account. On the opening day *'The attack starts, situation in our favour, Caumont taken, we move to Caumont and what a night, Jerry was shelling practically all night. Rowlands, bomb happy.'* The reference to Rowlands indicates the intensity of the bombardment they were receiving, as the phrase 'bomb happy' was soldiers slang for 'shell shock' correctly referred to as nervous exhaustion,(Bdr. Rowlands returned to the Regiment after a couple of days rest). This shelling continued for the next couple of days. On the 2nd August the Regiment moved forward, and witnessed again the devastation caused by their Gunners. Sgt Fletcher, *'Moved again, saw some horrible sights, quite a lot of good jerries on the road, all dead, terrible sights, had a bath in a stream'* Sgt Fletcher and the men often referred to enemy dead as *'good jerries'*. It's interesting to note here that although the men had seen some hard fighting and witnessed some pretty gruesome sights, they were not insensitive to the sight of dead soldiers. By 4th August the Regiment was positioned at St. Charles de Percy, and again, there was continued bewilderment at the chaos and carnage their guns had caused. They often admired how the Germans suffered it for so long.

The Gallop through France as the Gap Closes

The heavy fighting continued as the Division moved forward, and by the 11th August Operation "Bluecoat" was drawing to a close, finding the 181st at Monchamp in the Caen sector. On the 14th they moved to a marshalling area for their first rest since landing. The rest and refit took them to the Foret de Cinglais, on the banks of the River Orne. The weather was warm and sunny, and the respite was best remembered for its plagues of mosquitoes, many of the men receiving severe bites.

It was during the Caumont offensive that the 181st received their next Commanding

Officer when Lt/Col. RWB 'Dick' Bethell joined the Regiment. The Division also saw some changes. Due to wounds sustained during the fighting, Major General GHA. Macmillan, the Divisional Commander, was replaced by Brigadier CM. Barber, who came from 46th Bde. Known as 'Tiny' on account of his huge frame, and reputed to be have been the tallest man in the British Army at the time. In addition the very popular 'Bosun' Hilton was wounded, and replaced by Brigadier L. Bolton as C.R.A.

On 19th August after their well earned rest, the 181st were on the move again, in an effort to help drive the German Army towards Falaise in an attempt to stop them escaping from Normandy. The Division harboured North-West of Falaise but were not called into action, as the gap was closed. On the 24th Sgt Fletcher records, *'went down road of Falaise escape route, what a mess our RAF made, the vehicles all burnt out, plenty of dead Jerry around and what a stink, we are travelling fast to contact battle.'*

The Division was travelling as fast as possible in all manner of vehicles to catch up with those Germans who were in the area North-West of Paris. The gallop through France had begun, by way of Bernay. By the 26th Aug. the Regiment was harboured in Le Neubourg in preparation for the Seine crossing. The next day the Division commenced its crossing, but met with very little resistance, and only 178 Bty. was called into action in support of 227 Bde. Both units crossing at Port de Joie, just north of the loop in the Seine where the major part of the Division crossed.

The Division continued its pursuit of the battered German Army up through France, but failed to make contact, passing Amiens, Connelles, Arbacourt, Beauvais, on 6th September they crossed the Border into Belgium, at Lille. Here they experienced the full weight of Belgian hospitality as thousands thronged the streets to welcome the Liberators. Sgt Fletcher recorded for the 6th Sept: *'Crossed the Belgium border at Lille and what a reception, the people went wild, gave wine, apples, pears, and everything one could think of, they were certainly glad to see us, stayed the night at Halluein.'* It was a reception that few who were there would ever forget. It gave their hearts and morale a real boost, and made everything worthwhile, as the men realised what they were fighting for.

On 7th Sept. Sgt Fletcher wrote, 'Moved to a place called Harlebeke, we fired quite a few rounds at horse drawn artillery, our main job is to clear up pockets which have been left behind by our forward Troops. This incident is also mentioned in the History of the 15th Scottish Division, on page 123. *'That morning Capt (Jack) Cunis the F.O.O. from 177 Bty 181 Field Regt. arrived in Coutrai, to be greeted by a Captain of the Belgian Resistance, who led him to a tall block of flats, where they were mounted on the roof-garden. As the mist lifted the Belgian Capt pointed in the distance, there drawn up nose to tail were long columns of German transport, a strange array of country carts piled high with loot. It was a target that generations of Gunners dream of, the firing went on all day. Later on more enterprising spirits went out to round up prisoners and cut fresh steaks off the horses.'* But the shooting parties were soon to end as the reality of war was to rear its ugly head once again, in the waterways of Northern Belgium.

Chapter Ten

BACK TO WAR

On 12th September the Division arrived at the Abert Canal. A simple entry in Sgt Fletcher's Diary for that date gives no indication of the battle that was afoot. The retreating Germans had decided to make a stand here amongst the waterways of the Belgium/Holland border. Not since Normandy would the Division encounter such bloody fighting. Most of the men who were there have harrowing memories of the fighting in that sector which they always refer to as the Escaut Canal, but by far the biggest obstacles were taking the Gheel and Aart Bridgeheads over the Albert and Junction Canals. Sgt Fletchers Diary for that day: *'Arrived at Albert Canal, we fire a few rounds, Jerry pulled out 3 O'clock next morning'* Pulled back would have been the more appropriate word, had 'Fletch' known what was in store. After 3 days and nights of almost non-stop firing, and being constantly shelled themselves the situation was serious and could be sensed in the entry for the 16th: *'It's murder for our lads in front, the ali man is giving our lads hell, it can't be wondered at. Our O.P. party got hit with an 88mm., carrier out of action. The lads still holding on at heavy cost.'* It's worth noting that the 'Lads' are the Scottish Infantrymen in the front line, and not the members of his own Battery which gives some indication for the affection and respect that 'Fletch' had for the foot soldiers. On the 17th, for the second time, a major tragedy struck Charlie Troop as three of their Signallers were killed together whilst taking spare parts up to the Forward Observation Post. Two of them, Alf Adams and Jim 'Yanto' Evans had been with the Regiment since the early KSLI days, and the third, Gnr. E. Adams had joined the Regiment as an Artillery man at the conversion. Alf Adams had already lost his brother who was only 21 when he died of wounds while serving abroad. Alf himself had not long been married to a girl he had met while serving with the 6th Bn. KSLI when they were stationed in Lincoln. Alf and his Brother were both potters before being called to fight for their Country. Mr and Mrs Adams, who lived in Fenton Staffs had one other son who was also fighting for his Country somewhere overseas.

Sgt Fletcher, along with a party of volunteers, one of whom was my Dad, went out during the night to fetch the bodies in. They were given a temporary burial in the Churchyard at Gheel on the 18th September. L/Bdr Charlie Ashton, recalled being detailed to the party digging the graves, a grisly task as they dug into graves that had been there previously. After eight days of continuous fierce fighting around a tiny bridgehead held by 44 Bde. and 227 Bde, during which time they repulsed no less than 13 German counter-attacks and lost over 700 officers and men, the bridgehead was abandoned, and the Division moved westwards and continued through a position held by the 53rd Welsh Division. It was later learned that the sector was being held by General Student of the German 1st Parachute Army. It was he who organised all the German Troops fleeing from the west. These Troops were commanded by fanatical S.S. Officers and NCO's who had all manner of guns sent up from the nearby Artillery School at Bourg Leopold. The entry in Sgt Fletchers Diary, after just 7/8 days of horrendous fighting, 19th Sept 1944: *'Moved to a new position, thank God! Glad to get away from that place, arrived at a place called Moll, went out and had a drink, fired a few rounds.'* Tribute is paid to the Gunners of 'our' Regiment for their fine work, in this action on page 141 of the

Divisional history. *'No praise can do justice to the work of our guns throughout in this bridgehead fighting. Their fire was directed by a band of intrepid Forward Observation Officers of the 181st Field Regiment, who, from their observation post in the factory buildings kept an unending vigil under a ceaseless rain of high velocity shells.'* And in the words of Robert Woolcombe (p.154 Lion Rampant): *'Our Gunner OP's were shot out of the church spire, and off the factory roof - or at least they should have been, only they just stayed on! It was quite a sensation, when, in answer to your own voice a complete Field Regiment came crashing down onto some danger zone ahead of the company front'*. The only consolation for the heavy losses, were the many hundreds of enemy killed and tons of armour destroyed. No finer tribute could be made to the courage and fighting spirit of these 'Shropshire' boys when they were recognised by their Country. The Regiment was awarded 3 Military Crosses, and 3 Military Medals, plus a Distinguished Service Order won by the commanding Officer, Lt.Col. RBW. Bethell, for outstanding acts of gallantry in this action.

Leaving behind the wreckage at the Aart and Gheel bridgeheads, the Division moved northward, 22nd September finding them in a position just outside Eindhoven, having crossed the Dutch border the day before. On the 24th the Regiment passed through an area that had seen an American airborne landing just days earlier, the remains of hundreds of gliders scattered about the place, provided welcome shelter from the rain that had been falling for time, the gliders also provided the lads with a welcome change of diet as many of the them contained American rations.

On 27th September, the Regiment arrived at Best. An interesting entry from Sgt. Fletcher's Diary for the 28th showing a more human face of war: *'Jerry calls for two hours truce to get their wounded in, fierce fighting in their area, we ask them to surrender but they refuse, shelling us pretty often'* The Germans were asked on many occasions to surrender as the war got closer and closer to Germany, and their constant refusal in face of defeat, was extremely infuriating as the waste of life continued to its inevitable conclusion.

On 5th October, the Regiment was harboured in Beek and was pulled out of action for *'5 glorious days rest'* as Sgt Fletcher called it, after 100 days of being constantly in range of the enemy's guns, and travelling more than 400 miles. The rest period over, the 181st went into action once again this time in support of the 51st Highland Division who's objective was the town of S'Hertogonbosch, the barrage began at 3am, each gun firing about 200 rounds, Sgt. Fletcher, who went to A-sub gun after the death of Sgt Gunn on the Regiment's first action, in Normandy, reports that he fired 278 rounds during the barrage. S'Hertogonbosch was taken on the 27th October. On this date also the 15th Scottish Division had the honour of liberating the town of Tilburg, where in spite of shell damage to some of the houses they received a rapturous welcome, and to this day the Division has many memorials to its brave soldiers in and around the town, which has never forgotten the sacrifice that was paid for their freedom. The reception party was short lived for after only 48 hours rest the Regiment was called into action once again. News had reached Tilburg that German armed forces consisting of the 15th Panzer Grenadiers and the 9th Panzer Division had launched a strong counter-attack at the thinly spread American 7th Armoured Division at Asten. And this was threatening the British 2nd Army HQ at Helmond. From Sgt Fletchers diary 29th, October 1944: *'We move. The yanks have been pushed back 3 miles between Helmond and Eindhoven We are in the thick of it again, things not too good at the moment. Saw first Buzz Bombs.'* The German advance was halted by the 1st November, although the Regiment continued to meet stiff opposition and for the next

6 days they were bombed and shelled constantly. The Regiment remained in this area until 20th November.

Two days earlier the 181st lost its gallant Medical Officer Capt. Stuart Lowden RAMC. Well known to all of the Gunners, his death was a great shock, he was killed whilst trying to retrieve the body of his Medical Orderly L/Bdr. Marklew from a minefield. A letter from Lt. John Thomlinson of RHQ 181 Field Regiment, detailed the tragedy: *'L/Bdr. Marklew had been out into the minefield to recover casualties, when he was killed by a mine. Capt. Lowden. with a small party including Lt. Thomlinson, went into the minefield in an American half-track. After safely locating L/Bdr Marklew, the half-track was reversed up to the body, Capt. Lowden jumped down and took the body into his arms, as he was making his way back to the vehicle disaster struck, when the combined weights of both men triggered another mine, Capt. Lowden was dead by the time they reached the Regimental Aid Post.'* (See Appendix 4)

Battle Of The Rhineland

By 21st November the Regiment was dug in at Liessel, and pushing the Germans back to the River Maas, and taking the final strongholds, Sgt Fletcher continually complains of the dreadful weather conditions, rain almost continuously, not only making life very uncomfortable for the Troops but also holding up the momentum of the British advance. On 4th December one of the final German strongholds was broken in a big attack around Blerick. This attack was to become the subject of a War Office pamphlet so successful was it, and for the second time the regiment won a D.S.O. awarded to Capt. ADG.Shaw of D Troop 178 Bty. when during the attack, the leading company of the Infantry lost all its Officers. Capt Shaw quickly took control of the situation, and got the Infantry on to its target, whilst continuing to direct the fire of his own guns from his FOP. It is worth recalling that Capt Shaw was one of the original Officers who transferred from the 6th KSLI making him well qualified to lead an Infantry attack. The bad weather continued and by the 13th December the Germans had pulled back across the River Rhine. The British Army were now dug in on the west bank of the River Maas waiting for the weather to improve and making preparations for the assault crossing of the Rhine. On the 13th December the Division had a visit from Monty who had this to say: *"I remember very clearly visiting your Division in England when I came back from Italy. And I well remember your Division landing in Normandy when you came over just after D-Day. You were untried then, though you had some veterans with you. I remember the first time your Division went into battle at the River Odon, and remember feeling anxious that the Division should acquit itself well. One can't help feeling anxious at these times, though there is no need to. Your Division did very well and indeed, has never looked back since. You only have to look at the battle honours on the stage behind me - I have noticed well known names like Caumont - to realise how well you have done. I expect that today there are representatives of every unit in the Division. When you go back I want you to tell the others that I came here today and I think this Division has done awfully well, in this fighting no Division has done better, and it is a first class show. We did not expect anything else, but it is very creditable for all that."*

The appalling weather continued throughout December with no movement, though the Division was continuously bombed and shelled, giving back in like manner. The German lines only separated from the British by the stretch of water brought the two sides in close proximity, so close that many of the men I spoke to remembered hearing the Germans shouting abuse across the water. The most popular phrase - *'come over and fight you scotch b***s!'* Naturally, the Jocks were their equal when it came to insults. On Christmas Day the German Troops had a visit from a formation of Typhoons. The British soldiers loved the sight of these rocket firing planes diving and strafing the German lines gave a great boost to morale. It was three days later, on the 28th, that Sgt Fletcher and the rest of the Battery were able to celebrate Christmas, with a few parcels from home and a Christmas dinner, recorded as follows: *'Celebrated Christmas Day, had dinner in a barn, Jerry shelling to our left, a day I shall never forget.'* 1944 was drawing to a close and the men of 181 Field Regiment were looking forward to the day when they could all return home, having been in the thick of the fighting since June. The year was to go out with a bang as every German and British gun on both sides of the river went off at one minute before midnight, and the men who witnessed that night were never to forget it.

Preparations were now being made for the crossing of the River Rhine and the assault on the Siegfried line, which would carry the advance into Germany itself. On 17th January 1945 the Divisional Artillery was in support of the 7th Armoured Division attack on Roermond, and on the 24th they were back in Tilburg to come under command of the 1st Canadian Army, who were to control the crossing of the Rhine. By 4th. Feb The Regiment were harboured in Groesbeek, just east of Nijmegen, ready to move to their final position, before crossing and becoming part of the greatest Artillery assault of the war involving more than 1300 guns of every size. Here they remained until they moved into position on the 8th Feb., just south of Kranenburg, where a complex fire plan was executed in support of the infantry known as Operation 'Veritable'. Few who were there would forget the earth shattering roar as almost 1400 guns let fly at 5:30 am on the 8th February, greater even, than that of El Alamein. There was little rest for the men of the 181st, for apart from supporting their own 44 Lowland Brigade they were constantly called on to support the Division. The Regimental Diary for the the 12th February: *'Considerable firing in support of the Division'* and that on the day previous the Diary tells us the Regiment had fired over 4000 rounds. The attack moved forward quickly, so quickly that the guns were soon out of range, although the FOP's remained in position calling fire plans for other Field Regiments. Continuing to move forward the Gunners worked ceaselessly for the whole of February, taking the German towns of Kleve, on the 12th, Goch on the 16th/17th, and being in Bedburg by the 20th. From this area the Regiment supported, apart from their own Division, The 53rd Welsh, the 1st Canadian Armoured Division, the 3rd Canadian Division, the 3rd British Division, the 11th Armoured Division and the 51st Highland Division. At 2030 Hrs on 28th Feb the 181st were pulled out of action. During this period on 23rd February, Capt ADG. Shaw of D Troop 178/181 Field Regiment was singled out for mention in the Divisional History for bringing heavy Artillery bombardments on, Fasanenkath, Wolfberg, Bresaberg and Moyland.

On 1st March the Regiment returned once again to Tilburg for a rest and refit, and on the 6th. proceeded to Lummel and Hasselt in Belgium, for training in river crossing in preparation for the Rhine Assault. The river training was to take the Regiment up until 19th March, and during this time the 181st's Commanding Officer, Lt. Col. Dick Bethell, was posted to South East Asia Command (SEAC). His place was taken by Lt. Col. Pat Keene, who was the Regiments fourth C/O. He would lead the 181st Field Regiment all the way to Hamburg.

On 23rd March under cover of darkness the Regiment moved toward the River Rhine and took a position at Vynen, where they would harbour in preparation for their own crossing from a point called Xanten.

Crossing the Rhine

The Crossing was to be the grand finale, comparable to D-Day itself, pride of place in the centre was to be given to the 15th Scottish Div. On their right would be 1st Commando Bde. for the attack on Wesel, and on their left would be the 51st Highland Div., whose objective was the town of Rees. Under command of the 15th Div. for the crossing was; 4th Armoured Bde, 11th Army Group R.E., 5th Royal Berkshires and two Squadrons of the Royal Dragoons. In support were the specialised tanks or 'Funnies' of the 33rd Armoured Bde. On 24th March the Regiment was in action once again in support of their own 44th Lowland Brigade. After the crossing the Division was to link up with an airborne assault, which comprised the 6th British Airborne and 17th U.S Airborne Divisions who were due to land on the other side of the river just prior to the land assault, so timing was crucial. The debacle at Arnhem was still fresh in everyone's mind. Every man present was thrilled at the sight of the giant air armada as it passed over, right on time at 10:00hrs that morning, to begin the attack on the east side. For many the thrill soon turned to horror as they watched many of the gliders being hit by German anti-aircraft fire and their occupants being spilled out and sprinkled over the land to certain death, a memory that lives with many who were there to this day.

That day fortune smiled on the British Troops as the weather was very fine. Sgt Mottram of C Troop recorded the days events in his memoirs, *'Div. did assault crossing of the Rhine at 0200hrs, everything went according to plan, very few casualties.'* And for the 25th March: *'The Regiment crossed, in the afternoon. It was very exciting! the enemy were bombing and shelling. highlight of the day was watching the Airborne Divs. go into the attack at 10:00hrs. Regt. went into attack on the East side, ordered to support 44 Bde. The Regt. was first Field Regt. over the river - and got a good write up in the Newspapers. The Regt. was given an official congratulations by the CRA. and General Barber, the Divisional Commander.'*

Capt. John Meredith was with C Troop 178 Bty. which was the lead Troop. More memories from Gnr/Dvr. Charlie Spence: *"The half-tracks were shipped across on makeshift rafts, made up of long planks with short ones going cross-ways and fastened to lots of empty metal barrels. The half-tracks had to be carefully balanced to keep the raft level, they were powered by a small out board motor on each corner, each one controlled by a Royal Engineer, it seemed to take ages to cross."*

Time was of the essence, and it took only five hours for 44 Bde. to link up with both Airborne Divisions, Major Cumming-Bruce had ordered the pipes to lead the Brigade to let the Airborne Forces know they were on the way. So rapid was their progress, that by the 26th the 181st were well forward and was still the only Field Regiment across the Rhine. Sadly the operation wasn't totally without mishap, and the nightmare for all Gunners occurred, when two short shells knocked out almost half of two platoons of D Coy of 6 RSF. Among the dead was Sgt. E. Linard, a great pal of Sgt. Fletcher, 'Lin' was an ex-regular soldier who had served with both 6 KSLI. and 181 Field Regt. He was re-posted to the Infantry only weeks before, after complaining to an Officer that he was an Infantryman at heart. And later, during a tactical retirement after the crossing, the complete OP. party with the 131st Field Regt. were wiped out in an ambush.

The continued advance into Germany was met with fanatical resistance. The enemy were given the option to surrender at every opportunity. Their stubbornness was met with great force by the Jocks, furious at the continued pointless loss of life, as now the end was inevitable, and only a matter of time. Ueltzen, in particular, took 4 days to capture with great loss to the enemy, many of those trying to surrender were cut down by their own side.

On 27th March a bridgehead was established across a smaller but fiercely defended waterway, The river Issell (Ijssell) thought to be much smaller than it turned out, was taken in a brave head on assault by the men of the 6th Bn. Royal Scots Fusiliers, who waded chest deep to make the crossing, I have a gripping personal account written by one who was there, Fusilier Harry Holder 6 RSF. His experience is still vividly etched on his mind (see personal accounts). Ammunition supply across the river was now becoming a problem, as thousands of rounds were fired to prevent the enemy from re-forming. On 29th March, 4 days after the crossing, the Division was pulled out of action for a well deserved breather, and concentrated in a rear area on the East side of the Rhine. The Troops were now the occupying force in enemy territory, and as the weather broke they took to shelter, in civilian houses, and were told that no consideration was to be given to the German people in the matter of billets, not an easy task for the normally considerate 'Tommy'. The Division was later addressed by their Commander Royal Artillery, Brigadier Lyndon Bolton, who read out congratulatory messages, from Lt.Gen. Sir Miles Dempsey, Commander, British Second Army, Lt.Gen. NM. Ritchie, Commander British 12th Corps, and Maj. Gen. NM. Barber, Commander 15th Scottish Div.

Three days later the Division was on the move again, and had to catch up with the action, which had advanced over 70 miles, towards Munster. Here the 181st harboured, still many miles from the fighting. By 14th April they were back in action, in position at Holdenstadt for the attack on Ueltzen which was being held by Troops of the German S.S. The town fell 4 days later. 20th April found the Regiment at its final water obstacle, the River Elbe, and the next 9 days were spent making plans and preparations for its assault. Here the 181st were dug in at Artlenburg from where it was to launch its own barrage.

Chapter Eleven

THE FINAL DAYS

On 29th April 1945 the 181st Field Regiment went into action at Breitlingen in preparation for the Divisional assault on the River Elbe, the final water obstacle. Massive air cover was provided, courtesy of the RAF, as what was left of the Luftwaffe was out in force, The Regiment advanced towards Artlingen for greater accuracy, as the battle moved forward.

At 2100 hrs the following day, the Regiment prepared to make its own crossing, and this took place between 2200 and 2300 hrs on the 30th April. once again the 181st had the honour of being the first Field Regiment to cross, and were harboured on the east side of the Elbe at Julisberg the crossing complete. At daybreak the column was bombed and strafed by a jet propelled ME 262, 179 Bty. taking one casualty, though not fatal. They were quickly in action at Gulzow on the 1st May. Sgt Mottram recalled: *'The highlight of the day, seeing 5 Luftwaffe planes shot down by the RAF. And the guns of 119th LAA. Regt. RA. Morale was boosted 100% by this fine sight.'* The Division made swift progress and all three Batteries of the Regiment were in constant demand. By now the well rehearsed practice of 'On the Move' action had been honed to perfection in the previous battles, and the guns were made ready in minutes rather than hours.

For the first time, the War Diary of the 181st Field Regt. records on the 2nd May 1945. rather as a casual last minute entry, *'Rumours of surrender parleys very strong.'* The following day the 'no firing' order was received. 178 Battery was the last in action around the area Vorburg, before finally falling silent on the 4th May. The following day the whole of the Regiment was concentrated in the area Bargteheide.

The end of the fighting came swiftly, it must have been a massive relief not to be under the constant threat of bombardment, and the silence must have been deafening. Strangely not many of my old soldiers could recall their feelings on this day, save being thankful they survived and feeling sorrow for their fallen comrades, many of whom had been with the Regiment since the dark days of 1940, when they were members of the 6th Bn. KSLI. What honours they had achieved since then, what stories and memories they would hold. Major Dudley Shaw described it as an incredible anti-climax, mixed with relief, remembering taking the early days one at a time, mainly on instinct and adrenalin and at the end of each one being thankful he got through it unscathed. This did change he remembered, as the fighting went further into Germany and the end was close. He began to be a lot more calculated, not wanting to make a stupid mistake, that would cost him or his men their lives at this point, then being faced with the dilemma that perhaps a change in attitude might be for the worse, and make him more vulnerable.

The threat of being killed or injured was now over, and the main problem for the Officers was keeping the men fit and occupied after so many many months of intense danger and hard work. Football matches and Athletics meetings were being organised almost immediately and sport was high on the agenda. Quite soon after the surrender the Regiment was allocated occupational duties, which included rounding up Prisoners Of War and relocating displaced persons. Germany was in a chaotic state at this time and the task of keeping order and maintaining discipline was not easy. These duties continued into June and the Regiment was responsible for an area of some 220 square miles in the Kreis Lauenberg area covering all the towns and villages between Shwarzenbeck and Molln. The Batteries were located as follows. 177 Bty. Gudow; 178 Bty.Breitenfelde; 179 Bty.Grambeek; and RHQ. was at Woterson. Several selected men, mainly Drivers were detailed to the port of Kiel to assist in the surrender of the German Navy. 14th June was to record the first of the many sad events to come for the guns of this great Regiment. These great 25-pounders which had proved so lethal in the hands of the 'Shropshire Gunners,' which had taken such a decisive part in so many of the battles of North West Europe, and wreaked havoc amongst the enemy on so many occasions, and travelled so many many miles were cleaned and handed in to Ordnance.

Events moved quickly, and the first departures from the Regiment took place in August. Some Officers and men were posted to SEAC (South East Asia Command) to assist in the war that still raged in the Far East. Lt. John Thomlinson recalls receiving a telegram from the Regiment's previous CO. Dick Bethell, who had been posted as CRA. 23rd Indian Div. Having no wish to fight the Japanese, and looking forward to a relaxing time in Germany, his posting was fortunately curtailed by the A-Bomb. Occupational duties continued and many of the men were anxious to return to their homes and families. In preparation for the disbandment of the Regiment many of the men were posted to other Regiments, mainly to RA. units, but some went to Infantry. The oldest and longest serving men were the first to be demobilised. Many of the younger men were also posted on a scheme called 'Pickfords' so named after the removal company. These men were re-posted East, to help relieve the Troops ready for leave in the UK. Charlie Spence remembers spending his last few months in a transit camp in Deolali, India. *'No parades, a soldiers dream.'* He told me.

Keeping the men occupied was a constant problem, and Divisional games were organised along with football matches, one of which was against the 4th Bn. KSLI. in which many old acquaintances were renewed, as several men from the old 6th Bn. had been reposted there on the conversion back in 1942. The War Diary for December 1945 records. *'The whole of this month has seen the threat of disbandment looming'* A visit from the GOC., General Barber, to say goodbye to the Officers and men and thank them for their hard work, confirmed that the end was imminent, and shortly afterwards the 181st Field Regt left 15th Scottish Division. On 20th December 1945 the Regt. received a Christmas present it did not want, an army order, *'that it was to cease to be on the 9th January 1946'* a somewhat sad but inevitable end to a Regiment that was formed mainly out of civilians, who had become fine soldiers, and who had given everything for their country and the world's freedom from tyranny.

And so into history.......

There is no doubt that when people are thrown together to face adversity, a special bond of comradeship is forged, and mixed with the joy and relief that the war was over, came, what must have been a sense of the shared experience of an amazing adventure; the sort of journey that very few people will ever make in a lifetime. There must have been some regret, even amongst men hardened by sights and events that we hope never to see, at the passing of such an momentous experience, and the end of their huge family. This Regiment had achieved great things as part of the 15th (S) Div as history would subsequently record. I have read many accounts of the adventures of the Division, and the 181st Field Regt. has been singled out for special mention in each one. They were indeed, admired, loved and greatly respected by the Infantry which they supported so staunchly.

I shall leave the final paragraph to the pen of Capt. GW. Matthews the Regiment's Adjutant who had kept such a detailed War Diary throughout the campaign. The sense of pride and some sadness comes through in this final page of the Regimental War Diary.

January 1946:- This month has seen the final winding up of the Regiment. On Jan. 2nd the first large batch of men were sent away some 250 in all, it was hoped to get the remainder away on Jan. 9th. Owing to the delay in getting rid of all the stores, this proved impossible. The balance went away on Jan 12th. on which day the Batteries closed and their remaining Officers and men concentrated at RHQ. On Jan 15th. the audit board finished its work and on Jan. 16th. another batch of men and all Officers except the C.O., Adjutant, and Q.M. were sent away. On Jan 21st. a further batch of men were dispatched, leaving only some dozen to complete the final clearing up. On Jan. 23rd everyone departed with exception of the Adjutant and 4 O.R.'s these remaining five left on Feb. 24th. when the Regiment finally ceased to exist. So ended the existence of 181 Field Regiment RA. converted from the 6th K.S.L.I., the first Field Regiment across the Rhine in March 1945 and the first Field Regiment across the Elbe in April 1945.

Chapter 12

DRESS AND INSIGNIA

On joining the 6th Bn. the men were fortunate to be issued with the 1939 khaki battledress and greatcoat. Not for them the indignity of having to drill in their civvies with broomsticks, as was the experience for Capt. Philip Mulholland, who, before being commissioned into the KSLI, had joined the 11th Bn. Worcestershire Regt.

The new conscripts were originally issued with the (S.D.) service dress cap more commonly known to all soldiers as the 'cheesecutter'. This was replaced soon after formation by the field service cap (F.S.) cap which was more practical and could be turned into a winter warmer cap. These were issued in matching khaki, although the men could purchase another, in Infantry Green *'for walking out only'*. Strict instructions that these caps must be worn with point above the nose was ignored by most of the men who much preferred to wear them at a jaunty angle on the side of the head, a fashion which defied gravity. The famous KSLI cap badge was affixed and worn by all the members of the Battalion.

The Battalion had its own Shoulder Title, this was dark green, and in red letters the Title: 'KING'S SHROPSHIRE L.I..' The corners of the Title were rounded and I have seen only one example in its complete state. Most of the original issue were destroyed, as on conversion to Artillery there was a shortage of R.A. insignia and the men were instructed to remove the words KINGS and L.I. These were cut off at right angles to the bottom of the Title. I believe that my Dad is wearing this Title in the photo at the beginning of the book, at this stage the Regiment really was 'The SHROPSHIRE Gunners' and I'm pleased to say that I do have an example of the 'altered' title once worn by L/Bdr. Albert Smith.

After completing their initial training the men were posted to the Lincolnshire coast, where they came under command of the 204th Independent Infantry Brigade, who had their own insignia worn on the upper sleeve. This comprised, three small triangles formed into one large triangle, in the facing colours of the senior Battalions of the Brigade: Grey; 7th.Bn. Leicestershire Regt: Salmon Buff; 7th.Bn. South Lancashire Regt: Green; 12th.Bn. Sherwood Foresters. The whole was surrounded by a blue border.There were no further changes until the men converted to their Artillery unit in March 1942.

The whole of the newly formed Artillery Regiment were frustrated to find that the War Office were not ready for them, and there was hardly any Artillery insignia to go round. There was a mixture of cap badges issued, these were the familiar Artillery 'gun' badge together with Artillery 'bomb' badge. In recognition of their Infantry background the men were allowed to retain their original F.S. cap, but new arrivals to the Regiment were issued with the Artillery F.S. in Artillery scarlet and blue. Officers from the old 6th KSLI. who chose to transfer to Artillery were allowed to retain their green infantry lanyards and their KSLI buttons on their service dress. The scarlet arm-of-service strip worn by the infantry was replaced by the Artillery, scarlet and blue strip. The shoulder title was initially as described above before being replaced by the familiar Royal Artillery title, scarlet lettering on a dark blue background.

Shortly after the conversion and the men's initial training, the Regiment was transferred to Northumberland for gunnery practice, where they came under Northern Command and the men had a further badge to add to their growing collection. This was a triangular cloth badge in blue with a green apple in the centre, adopted for its association with the G.O.C. Sir Ronald F. Adam. Once again close scrutiny of my Dad's photo shows him wearing this badge on his upper sleeve. There is some evidence that this badge was only worn by those men attached to H.Q, but I have no confirmation of this. On moving North the Regiment had a new C.O., Lt.Col. EO. Herbert. He thought it fitting that the Regiment's Infantry ancestry should be officially recognised and this came in the form of a unique regimental badge of distinction an embroidered infantry bugle, in gold on a dark green background. This badge was worn by every member of the Regiment. The ex-KSLI men were immensely proud of it. but not so the 'Gunners' who joined the Regiment after conversion. They had there own military tradition to uphold. But military backgrounds were soon forgotten and the Regiment fought together under the same banner. This Badge is clearly visible in many of the photographs.

Whilst serving in Northumberland, the Regiment came under command of the 15th (Scottish) Division which saw another, final, change of insignia. This was the Divisional sign, a change from the sign the Division fought under during The Great War. The Fifteenth letter 'O' was retained but the red 'Scotch' was replaced by the rampant lion of Scotland within the 'O', on a gold background, the whole mounted on a black patch. This sign was worn by all the men in the Division, below the shoulder title. I have many photos of ex-personnel showing their Regimental and Divisional insignia. As a final touch, in June 1943, the men were issued with headgear of a more Scottish flavour. The cap T.O.S. the Tam O' Shanter, in khaki, handed out with great ceremony in exchange for the cap F.S. As witnessed by some of my photos, many of the men wore this cap with great finesse, standing up and lying down in all the right places. Alas, many of the men never quite got the hang of it, and it's easy to see why it was affectionately nicknamed the 'Cowpat'. I have been able to identify many background figures in photographs by the style in which they wore their Tam.

The Officers of the Regiment wore a smaller version of the Tam known as the Balmoral Bonnet, in grey. Affixed to the left hand side of both caps, on top of patch of scarlet and blue was the Artillery 'bomb' badge which was worn by Officers and other ranks. Photographic evidence shows that the men of the Regiment very often wore their Tams in battle, although it is certain that under bombardment they would have worn their steel helmets. This was the insignia worn by the 6th KSLI /181st Field Regiment during the campaign in N.W. Europe and afterwards in Germany with the Army of Occupation, until disbandment in 1946

In addition to these badges, tradesmen would wear a proficiency badge, after passing a trade test. These would include, Signallers, Drivers, Driver/Mechanics, Gunlayers, etc. all in various grades, each grade of course giving the soldier a small rise in pay.

Chapter 13

PERSONAL ACCOUNTS

Sgt. Dick Fletcher - A personal account

Sgt Richard (Dick) Fletcher from Leominster joined the King's Shropshire Light Infantry, as a young man in 1932 and was enlisted into the 1st Battalion. After serving his time with the Colours he returned to civvy street and was re-enlisted at the beginning of the war into the newly formed 6th Battalion. As an ex-Regular he was quickly made up to the rank of corporal, and helped form the core of NCO's and Officers whose task it was to shape the newly conscripted men into soldiers.

Sadly Dick died in 1991 and I did not meet him personally, although he did call at my childhood home in Birmingham along, with Percy Lewis to visit my dad after the War. It was Percy who introduced me to his daughter, Val. Showing a great deal of interest in my project, she was happy to hand me a box containing her late fathers service momentoes, included amongst the badges and papers was a Diary written in pencil in an old exercise book. Every soldier knew that keeping a Diary was strictly against regulations lest it fell into enemy hands. However, many men did, and these have provided historians and researchers with a real insight into the day-to-day lives and thoughts of the ordinary soldier, untouched by the romanticism and editorial extravagance of publishers. For some unexplained reason the Diary finishes on New Years Eve 1944 and is actually finished off with a tribute to his comrades, indicating that he had no intention of continuing recording the rest of his adventure.

Although an Infantryman Dick Fletcher was posted to 181st Field Regiment when the 6th Bn. converted and he became a well respected, reliable Artilleryman rising to the rank of Sergeant and being awarded a Commander-in-Chief's Certificate for his valuable service. Remembered by his ex-comrades and Officers as a 'tough, rough and ready soldier'. His Troop Captain, John Meredith, thought very highly of him and greatly valued his experience and toughness in difficult situations. Initially posted to 177 Bty, he was transferred to 178 Bty at the request of Captain Meredith to replace Sgt. Gunn who was killed just before the Regiment went into action. He joined C Troop where he remained for the rest of the fighting.

It's clear from his diary that Sgt Fletcher, was one those who failed to get off the ship before the storm set in, and his first few entries record his time on board:

June
13th: Set sail from Albert Dock, anchored in the Thames for night awaiting convoy.
14th: Set sail, fairly quiet crossing, had plenty of luck at cards.
15th: Saw coast of France, anchored 1/2 mile off the beach, too rough to disembark Won £8.
16th: Still on board sea getting worse, likely to be quite a while, lads are fed up and a little seasick.
17th: No improvement, rations running short, no cigs fed on bully beef.
18th: Still on board, not a cig between us, bully and biscuit again, Jerry welcomed us with a firework display dropped one incendiary bomb on the boat the lads first experience in battle, a little panicky.

19th: Situation critical, still too rough to get ashore, no rations.

20th: Attempted to unload guns and vehicles on raft what a job still too rough.

21st: Unloaded all from ship onto raft, situation still serious.

22nd: Woke to find the raft has broke loose from ship, all guns lost together with our kit, lucky I did not stay on board as I intended.

23rd: Small boat arrives with rations, we eat and smoke, still too rough to leave the boat.

24th: At last, we are away in an LCT. What a sight on the beach, join Regiment at the assembly area, lads thought we had went down.

25th: We go into action at Bronay, our first casualties, Arthur Gunn, Ginger May, McMorland, a bad start.

26th: We fire our first barrage, about 500 rounds, no response from Jerry, attack going well, Major Brown brings in our first prisoners.

27th: Enjoy myself hunting snipers, had to keep our heads down, bullets flying all over the place.

28th: Moved to a cornfield, and what a place, it was like hell on earth, Jerry tanks broke through, things not going too well, fired the biggest barrage that has ever been fired at night, things are improving a little, dead tired no sleep for 48 hours.

29th: Attack going well, Jerry still sending shells over, snatched two hours sleep, Jackie got it through the ankle, Capt. Cory-Wright killed, me and Jim found two good Jerries.

30th: Heavy firing all day, the lads and myself dead beat but not a complaint from any of them, situation still in hand trouble from snipers captured 4 that day.

July

1st : Went for 5 days rest, needed it badly, saw first bomber raid East of Caen, managed to get a little black bread.

2nd: Feel grand a good night's sleep, found a cafe, had a few drinks, pretty quiet night, had a look round for our Jim, no luck.

3rd: Sunny day, general clean up, managed to get some milk, butter and cheese. Night was not so quiet, another firework display by Jerry.

4th: Busy day again today, getting ready for front line again.

5th: Moved to St. Mauvieu, everything down to the ground and what a stink, dead stock all around us, fired quite a few rounds.

6th: Had a look around, found the grave of a French woman who had been raped and murdered by Jerry, the lads buried her in the garden. (RAF Carpiquet)

7th: It has arrived at last! bread, the first we have had since arriving in the country, fired nearly all day.

8th: Found a barrel of cider, had a bit of a do, soon found out it wasn't poisoned.

9th: Fired all day, no rest for the wicked!

10th: Big barrage, situation in hand.

11th: Another slice of bread (received) Jeans present, fired quite a few shells.

12th: Very quiet day.

13th: Not much doing.

14th: Moved to Mouen, it was like hell on earth Jerry gave us a good reception with his bombers, admit I was a little scared.

15th: Night attack, my gun was out of action, Jerry giving us a pretty rough time, all dreading 11:15 tonight.

16th: Another night attack, workshops next morning, had a bottle of gin and got drunk, thought my time had come, Jerry bombers over again.

17th: Jerry continually shelling sending one over our position every 3 minutes, one fell right in my gun pit flames were 20 feet high, young Titch got it in the leg, a day I shall never forget.

18th: 4:30 Jerry shelling us again, 4000 bomber raid North - East of Caen, lucky day, armour piercing shell came right through a tree which I was stood under, his bombers were over and was dropping them pretty close, took to our slit trenches.

19th: Busy day, Jerry machine gunned us, grazed my wrist very lucky no damage done another visit from Jerry.

20th: Jerry still sending them over, met our George after walking about 10 miles, start of so called rest.

21st: still in same position, shall be glad to get away from here, fired 21 rounds went to see our George.

22nd: Getting ready to move and are we pleased, Jerry still shelling, bombers over again, our kid goes up the front line again.

23rd :We move, and what a relief, to Balleroy on the American sector, like going from hell to heaven, how quiet it seems, it don't seem natural.

24th: Quiet day nothing unusual, plenty of digging, managed to get a little butter.

25th: Still quiet, plenty of digging, another slice of bread.

26th: Nothing unusual went to bath at Balleroy.

27th: Fired a few rounds, our net caught fire, more digging.

28th: Jerry shelled cross-roads by our positions, his bombers were out at night dropping flares, and a few bombs in the far distance.

29th: Getting ready to support the Yanks in their attack on Caumont.

30th: The attack starts, situation in our favour, Caumont taken, and we moved to Caumont and what a night, Jerry was shelling practically all night, (George) Rowlands bomb happy.

31st: Moved again, shelled by Jerry. Yanto and Smith very lucky, nearly got hit with Jerry machine-gunning, had a rabbit for supper, his bombers out again.

August

1st: Busy day cleaning up a pocket, Jerry over again.

2nd: We moved again, saw some horrible sights, quite a lot of good Jerries on the road, all dead, some terrible sights, had a bath in the stream.

3rd: Fired quite a few rounds, managed to get a drop of cider and milk, civilians pleased to see us, all you hear from the children is - *"cigarette for papa."*

4th: Saw us at a place, St. Charles de Percy, saw the damage we done with our airburst killed quite a number of Jerries, missed quite a bit of money, better luck next time.

5th: Fired over 100 shells, things going well, will soon have them on the run, buried a few Jerries, business pretty good.

6th: Still plenty of firing haven't had our clothes off for twenty nights, could do with a good nights sleep, weather lovely.

7th: Bank Holiday Monday, a lovely day, no one knew it was Bank Holiday Monday till late Tuesday.

8th: Still at same position, got quite a lot of Jerry equipment, Hardy joined us.

9th: Right browned off, packed up to move and it was cancelled, had to unpack all our kit again, some nice language used. Going not too good our Infantry withdrawing Everecy.

10th: Moved again to a place near Estry, fired all day holding the enemy, pretty tough going, managed to get a few hours sleep in the morning.

11th: Back to Caen sector, Monchamp, didn't fire much, they are trying to close the Falaise Gap.

12th: Still in same position, didn't fire much, Yanks making good progress.

13th: Prepared to move, our bombers over in 100's.

September

1st: Orders to move cancelled, we were going to Amiens, trying to make contact with Jerry. Brest and Pas-de-Calais captured, Americans 2 miles from Belgium border.

2nd: Went for a bath in River Seine had a swim, British and Canadians across Belgium border.

3rd: Moved from Conelles went 15 miles to harbour area, still failed to contact Jerry he must be running like a rabbit. Pas-de-Calais had severe shelling. Jerry evacuating his flying bomb sites.

4th: Left for Arbacourt about 15 miles away, slept there for the night.

5th: Moved to Beauvais. saw quite a lot of prisoners

6th: Crossed the Belgium border at Lille, and what a reception the people went wild, gave wine apples, pears and everything one could think of, they were certainly glad to see us. We stayed the night at Halluein.

7th: Moved again to a place called Harlbeke, we fired quite a few rounds at horse drawn artillery, our main job is to clear up pockets left behind by our forward Troops.

8th: Still at Harlebeke, ordered to move, we are now well inside Belgium, things now moving pretty fast, we are moving tonight.

9th: We arrive in Danty, working all day cleaning the gun, did all my washing, reports that Jerry are getting out quick.

10th: Moved to harbouring area, we travelled North - West of Brussels, stayed at a place called Hum-Beek, nice little village had a bath.

11th: Still at Hum-Beek, plenty of Mademoiselles around the camp, went out for a drink at night, managed to get a few eggs, we are going to support the 50th. Division.

12th: Arrived at Albert Canal, we fired a few rounds, Jerry pulled out at 3 0'clock next morning.

13th: Moved to other side of Albert Canal, we met up with Jerry again, he slung plenty of 88mm. at us, We fired all last night.

14th: We fired again last night, and all day today, Jerry started started shelling us again, we got to keep our heads down or else.

15th: Another night and day of firing, KOSB. and RSF. going in to attack, our RAF. firing their rockets giving them hell, we hold bridgehead over Escaut Canal.

16th: It's murder for our lads in front, the Ali man is giving us hell, it can't be wondered at our OP. got hit with an 88mm. Carrier out of action. The lads still holding on at heavy cost.

17th: A day I shall never forget, Yanto went to carry wireless set over river - lost his life, a grand lad. Also Adams killed and two wounded. Volunteered to fetch him in at night time, what a place pouring down with rain, like a creepy film you see at the pictures. Managed to get his body back after carrying him 3/4 mile, a night that will always live in my memory. Saw airborne going to Arnhem.

18th: I get Yanto's and Adams' bodies back and gives them as decent a burial as possible under the circumstances. Buried them in blankets at Gheel churchyard in Belgium several Canadians were buried same time - some grave!

19th: Moved to new position, thank God! glad to get from that place, arrived at place called

Moll, went and had a drink, fired a few rounds

20th: Still at same position, fired a few rounds, haven't heard much news, plenty of civilians around all looking for souvenirs, some nice girls to.

21st: Moved again, 131 Regt. took our positions over. We move over the Dutch border in the dark, the lads still pushing on.

22nd: Well into Holland, passed quite a big place Eindhoven, passed Philips wireless factory, raining heaven hard, in position just outside Eindhoven, at one hours notice to move.

23rd: Moved, rain heavy, another Airborne landing, fired a few rounds we are hard on Jerries heels.

24th: Moved, near a place called Best, hundreds of gliders were in the fields near us, got quite a lot of cigs and Yankee rations, needed them as our rations were terrible.

25th: Still in same position, living on Jerry rations. Found a few good Jerries, business pretty good, managed to get a treat for Jean. Jerry reported in the woods to our right. Jerry has started his games again, but if he sends one shell at us, we send about 10 back.

26th: We start to dig gun pits, didn't have time for a wash, pouring with rain, but the war must go on, dead tired.

27th: Still at same position, finished gun pit, done quite a lot of firing, pouring with rain managed to keep dry in the gliders.

28th: The place we are at is called Best, we managed to get quite a lot of kit here, I went for a bath to Eindhoven, lovely bath, rations still terrible.

29th: Jerry calls for two hours truce to get their wounded in, fierce fighting in their area, we ask them to surrender but they refused, shelling us pretty often.

30th: Moved to a new position digging gun pits all night, rained, pouring all night, still not a decent night's sleep and the rations are stinking. Dead tired, fired quite a few rounds, raining like hell, wet through in and out all night.

October

1st: Rude awakening Jerry shelling our position, we were all very lucky, pieces of shrapnel went through the tent no casualties.

2nd: Moved to a place called Beek for 5 glorious days rest, and we need it badly, a good nights rest will do us the world of good.

3rd: A good nights rest, feel champion, work hard all day. Went to pictures at Helmond quite a good show, no smoking allowed in the pictures it was quite a change for us.

4th: Worked all day, on guard at night nothing much happened. I think all the village came up to see us. All we could get from them was " cigarettes for papa" They got cigs for papa,- 1 Gilda a time. 1/10½

5th: Worked all day had ½ hours gun drill, afternoon in Eindhoven, tried to buy a present for Esther, no luck, went to pictures.

6th: Plenty of work all day, went for a bath at Eindhoven, lovely bath had swimming pool attached.

7th: Still hard at work, expecting to move, cancelled, our bombers going over Germany, nothing much to write about.

8th: Still at rest, played football against Dutch civilians won 3 -1. News still good Americans less than 10 miles from Cologne. The lads are still pushing on.

9th: Rest period finished, went to support 30 corps can see Seigfried line, fired quite a few rounds, pouring with rain.

10th: Still raining digging hard all day, soaking wet through and hungry, preparing for big push,

Yanks warn Germans to get out of Aachen.

11th: Still preparing for big barrage, Jerry started sending his shells over, things not to healthy. Rain ceased.

12th: We fire our barrage, things going pretty well, South Lancs. Gained their objectives, the attack going well. Fired 278 rounds, quite a number of prisoners.

13th: Still in same position, send digging party forward, move cancelled, raining hard all day.

14th: Our bombers going over in strength, had news that I was going to Brussells in the morning.

15th: Wet through, stayed with 177 Bty. the night, what a fuss they made, hadn't seen them for quite a while, satisfied my hunger, still raining.

16th: Went to Brussells, what a place had a smashing time, plenty of women there, it looked like peace time, couldn't get a drink in peace women all over you.

17th: Good nights rest even a cup of tea in bed, went sight seeing in the morning shopping in the afternoon, can buy anything there - bought Esther a bracelet.

18th: My good time has come to an end, I go back this afternoon, like going from heaven to hell but I have enjoyed myself, arrived back at 11 O'clock.

19th: The Troop having a rest at Beek., went to pictures in afternoon, saw Fanny by gaslight.

20th: We move, 51st Div. need help we support them we are now at S'Hertogonbosch at least not far from there. The lads are going to put in a big attack.

21st: Prepare for barrage, raining hard all day wet through again could do with a good nights sleep.

22nd: We fire our barrage at 3 o'clock in the morning attack going well, fired quite a lot of ammunition.

23rd: We fire another barrage, today news good, Infantry advanced to within 3 miles of S'Hertogonbosch .

24th: Things going well we move forward under observation from the enemy, news good we have entered the outskirts of S'Hertogonbosch.

25th: Weather is better, we move to within 13 kilometres of Tilburg at a place called Best this place had been retaken by Jerry but we soon got them out of it again. Could do with a good nights sleep and a square meal, living on Jerry rations.

26th: Moved forward through Best, what a mess we made of it everything down to the ground. Jerry still giving ground.

27th: Saw us firing into Tilburg, We capture Tilburg also S'Hertogonbosch is in our hands. Saw all the collaborators getting rounded up and having their hair trimmed. A good reception.

28th: We are still advancing, we had good reception in Tilburg even though we knocked their homes about a bit. Had a good sleep in a farmer's barn.

29th: We move the Yanks have been pushed back 3 miles between Helmond and Eindhoven, we are in the thick of it again. Things not too good at the moment. Saw first buzz bombs.

30th: News a little better, we have stopped their advance, Jerry bombers over at night.

31st: We are at a place called Asten, quite a nice position near a house, the old couple moved out, nearly knocked their house down when we fire our guns, feel sorry for them, fired quite a few rounds. Yanks moved out.

November

1st: Still at Asten we have stopped their advance and they are now withdrawing. Jerry over again at night.

2nd: We moved again to another position a few miles away, don't like this position in the middle of a ploughed field. Our bombers were over.

3rd: Digging gun pits, Jerry shelled us no casualties, meeting stiff opposition plenty of firing. Food is terrible.

4th: We are still meeting stiff opposition, our gun is out of action, so we get a couple of hours rest.

5th: Gun still out of action, valve gone in action that day, fired a barrage quite a lot of supercharge fired.

6th: Didn't get no rest Jerry bombing nearly all night, news is pretty good south Holland nearly cleared of Jerries. Food still lousy.

7th: Nothing much happened today, fired a few rounds, sent a parcel away to Esther.

8th: Quiet day today went to baths at Asten, General Barber paid us a visit, complimented A Sub on their slit trenches.

9th: Still at same position, fired a few rounds, nothing much doing, raining, pouring.

10th: We move to Asten for general clean up. Sent Esther £15. Had good nights sleep in a loft.

11th: Still at Asten, Went to Helmond to cinema quite a good show, digging party to new position.

12th: We move to new position, Jerry shelled us 2 hours after we had been there, pretty close but no casualties. Preparing for big attack.

13th: Still waiting for the word go, fired a few rounds that day and prepared ammunition for the attack.

14th: We prepare and fire smoke, only to discover that attack is a fake, fooled Jerry alright the attack went in to our right, going well.

15th: We fired a big barrage in supporting 53 Div. The attack going well, we made ourselves comfortable made a fireplace in our tent, what a change quite like home.

16th: News still good the front is now nearly 400 miles long, saw buzz bombs, launching base can't be far from here.

17th: Sent digging party to new position, Jerry shelling to our right, went for a bath to Asten, dead tired we are 10 miles from Seigfried line Jerry guns sending plenty of shells over.

18th: Still in same position, 2 casualties, Marklew and the Medical Officer killed by mines got to be very careful were you walk round here, one false move and you have had it.

19th: Still in same position, our bombers still going over in great strength, moved late at night

20th: Arrived in new position, rained heaven hard all buildings down to the ground. Water filling our slit trenches, right browned off.

21st: Moved to new position dug in as usual, place we are at now, Liessell, fired a few shells in Venlo direction.

22nd: Supported 12th Armd. Div. attack going well, Americans capture Metz.

23rd: Still in same position, raining like hell, fire a few rounds, news still going well.

24th: Very quiet today, we may move to a new position, still raining hard.

25th: We move to a new position, to a place called America, rained heaven hard, awful, wet through.

26th: We are in a position just outside of Horst, still raining. 2nd. Army fought a big battle at Geilendirch. French have crossed the Rhine.

27th: Still in same position, news good, good reports that the Yanks have taken Strasbourg. Raining like hell.

28th: Maintenance all day, rained all day. Had new Battery Commander, fired a few rounds at night. Managed to get a few eggs.

29th: Captain Meredith awarded the MC. Aspley the MM. they deserve it. Moved to a place west of Venlo. Took over from 49th Div.

30th: Still in same position, plenty of digging, went to cinema in afternoon at Horst, bitter cold in pictures. Jerry shelling to our right and left.

December

1st: It looks as though we are here for the winter, start to make ourselves comfortable Jerry still shelling, we firing a few rounds, news pretty good.

2nd: Ginger posted to R - Sub. Smith made up L/Bdr. Fired a few rounds, raining again.

3rd: We support infantry in a big attack around Blerick driving Jerry the other side of the Maas, attack going well, gained 1st objective in good time, our nearest weapons were in support.

4th: Situation in hand closing in on Blerick driving Jerry back across the River Maas. Raining like hell, Americans pushing into Germany.

5th: Still at same position, heard good news about leave. Paddy got killed by a mine, 50 yds from our gun, a grand lad.

6th: Made an air raid shelter, it looks as though we shall need it, Jerry shelling to our left and right ever since we arrived here.

7th: Plenty of digging today raining like hell, heard we are going out for a rest, we need it badly.

8th: News good the Seigfried line has been broken into in three places, still no rest.

9th: Went to Asten for a bath, still raining like hell. Jerry shelling to our right.

10th: Still raining like hell, our sleeping quarters collapsed, some nice language, a horse got blowed to pieces by a mine. plenty of civvies evacuating Blerick. Reminds me of Berwick.

11th: We move back to our old position, rained like hell as we moved in, glad to get back.

12th: Get settled in our old position, like going back home, still raining.

13th: The Jerry have withdrew all his Troops across the Rhine, all we do now is sit tight and hold them, news still good down south.

14th: We hear we are going out for a rest again, could certainly do with it, raining like hell again.

15th: Lads prepared next area but it looks as though we have had it, thought as much news have just come through, rest cancelled, no rest for the wicked.

16th: Gun down to L.A.D. Plenty of Jerry dive-bombers over had a go at one with a bren gun, hit it three times but failed to fetch it down.

17th: Gun still in L.A.D. Dive bombers over, and have been all day. 190th Field Regt. got bombed, thought we were in for it.

18th: News have just reached us that Jerry have started a big offensive down south, they have advanced 30 miles into Belgium. Jerry dive bombers over again.

19th: We move to harassing fire position at Maasbree fired quite a few rounds Jerry over again

20th: We move to new position, we dig ourselves in, news not good down south Jerry still advancing.

21st: Still at harassing fire position, we fired all last night. Jerry shelling in front of us.

22nd: We move back to old position, a good job too, weather pretty good, bitter cold, frosty but dry, shelling to our left.

23rd: News that Jerry is attempting a breakthrough, double our guard.

24th: Intelligence reports, 2.000 Paratroops in Venlo, we must stop them at all costs, we have 100% stand-to, not much hope of a decent Xmas.

25th: Wouldn't know it was Xmas Day, same as any other day to us. If Jerry tries to breakthrough what a shock he will get we are all prepared, no attempt at a breakthrough yet we are still waiting patiently, bitter cold, white Xmas. Our Typhoons visit, playing hell with Jerry.

26th: Our bombers have been over this morning wishing Jerry a merry Christmas, sent a few shells over, looking forward to a letter mail just arrived, no letter for Dick, what a Christmas, hope Esther has a better one than this, roll on next Christmas lets have some nuts. Still 100% stand-to.

27th: Woke up with a thick head got drunk last night, drank all the spirits I had, lads say I got up to some nice tricks, was going to swim the River Maas and bring a few Jerries back. Fired a few rounds on enemy mortars.

28th: Still at same position, fired a few rounds still 100% stand-to, no rest for the wicked, went up to the front to see Lin. Celebrated Xmas Day, had dinner in a barn, bitter cold day, Jerry shelling on our left, a day I shall never forget.

29th: Moved to harassing fire position, bitter cold digging slit trenches, up all night.

30th: Came back for 24 hrs. glad to be back, Jerry shelled our harassing fire position.

31st: A night that will always live in my memory, all was quiet from 11:30 until a minute to 12. after that it was just like hell, for about 20 minutes everything went mad, there were shells and bullets whizzing all over the place, bombs were dropping away to our left, sky was like the illuminations at Blackpool. I was one that was glad to see the new year in, it was bitter cold, we helped to make as much noise as possible by sending 10 high explosive shells into Germany. We had no sleep last night. This time last year Esther was with me in Harrogate.

For whatever reason, Sgt. Fletchers diary finished at this point, with a final 'memo' in which he pays a fine tribute to the men he served with, this makes it appear that it was intentional, and why he never continued writing will always be a mystery. He stayed with the Regiment until its break-up, when he transferred to 121 LAA Regt.

Memo:

In addition to all this we were living, eating and sleeping in slit trenches, tonight is my 50th without a decent sleep, we could never settle down and be sure of a good nights sleep as we were always ready to be called out at a moments notice when the situation arose. Have done guard duty every night this past six months, no joke in weather like this, bitter cold.

We spent Christmas stand-to in our slit trenches, as Jerry was expected to try and break through our position, what a shock he would have got if he had come. Our entertainment has been limited, sometimes we are lucky if 1 out of 14 of us goes to the pictures about once a week. The food we used to get was stinky, we were living on captured Jerry rations, it's a good job I still had both my hands otherwise we should have seen more meal times than meals.

I have seen some horrible and also pathetic sights since I have been out here, have been pretty lucky myself up to the time of writing this. Got a good set of lads, no matter what the situation is like or how much work they got to do, never a complaint will you get from them, Jerry could send all he have got but it will never break the spirit of the boys. To see these lads walk around England you wouldn't think they would harm a fly, but when trouble arises they fight like tigers.

John Meredith 178/181 Field Regt R.A. - A personal account

With the dark days of Dunkirk still in the very near past, the Summer months of 1940 saw the birth or rebirth of many units hurriedly mobilised to meet the apparently imminent threat of invasion.

June and July of that year saw among these many others the rebirth of the 6th. (Pals) Battalion of the King's Shropshire Light Infantry. By the end of July intakes of men from Shropshire, Herefordshire and the Potteries brought the reborn Battalion up to something like full strength in men if not in Officers and trained N.C.O's, and the training of the unit was begun under the oak trees of the Sherwood Forest at Thoresby Park.

After only a few weeks a move was made to more suitable, (and less dusty) quarters at Welbeck Abbey where each company carried out its first exercise - the never to be forgotten attack on Langworth Mill.

By October the Battalion was considered to be sufficiently trained to move to the coast - and its first operational role was the guarding of the Lincolnshire beaches in the area of Gibraltar Point, south of Skegness. As members of the old Lincolnshire Division we moved up and down the coast, North and South of Skegness, and by early 1942 every man in the Battalion had a very fair knowledge of the County - as moves were frequent - and our role varied. In addition to guarding the Coast, we had spells of training inland and did a share of Aerodrome defence, among spots visited by one Company or other being Spilsby, Skegness, Mablethorpe, Wainfleet, Louth. Borth and many smaller towns and villages too numerous to mention.

Towards the end of 1941 rumours as to the future of the Battalion were numerous - the most popular, perhaps, being that we were shortly to leave for India, but in February the news came out at last - we were to become Gunners. This meant goodbye to the regular Officers of the Battalion and to many other good friends - but when the 181st Field Regt, RA. eventually came into being near Melton Mowbray in Leicestershire, it was good to see so many of the Shropshire lads with us, and at least we were allowed to wear the Shropshire "Bugle" on our shoulders, and proud we were to do so.

On looking back on the short life of the 6th. Battalion, as such, three things must remain very strongly in the memory of all the old members of the Unit. They are the Football Xl, the Greyhound Racing, and the Marches by Platoons from the Coast to Shrewsbury.

The Commanding Officer, Lieut. Col. R.B.S. Munn, M.C., was a great believer in sport as a way to physical fitness and as a morale builder. The Soccer Xl, therefore was given ample opportunity to train and practice, and, numbering as it did such men as Tudor,(of West Bromwich Albion fame now with Wrexham), Paddy Mills of Leeds United, (Paddy was killed by a mine at Massbree in Holland), Franklin of Blackpool and Lilley of Birmingham, it is little wonder that before long it had become the pride of the Battalion, and one of the best, if not the best Unit side in the Army at that time. If my memory serves me correctly their only defeat was at the hands of an R.A.F. side at Skegness, who, on learning of the record of the Shropshire footballers turned out so strong a side that an English International, by no means a spent force was numbered among their reserves!

Quite early in its career the Battalion became possessed of a number of Greyhounds - partly as Mascots, and partly as raisers of revenue for the P.R.I. The dogs were a mixed blessing, though the race meetings certainly produced very useful funds and attracted large crowds including a fair number of the betting fraternity - but the unfortunates, myself included, whose role in life it was to run the "Tote", were not broken-hearted when an overwhelming number of summonses on the score of "no licenses" etc. brought about their downfall.

The "Shrewsbury Marches" were, in the first place the idea of Lieut. J.C. Wright, who, after leaving us for the 1st Battalion and being mentioned in Despatches for his excellent work on Night Patrols in North Africa, had the misfortune to be *"put in the bag."*

Great enthusiasm reigned in the Unit as each Platoon to leave on its 150 mile march tried to beat the previous record time set up, and on the eve of our conversion into Gunners I shared with 2/Lieut Len Sturley of Hereford the honour of leading the winning Platoon - a composite one from Head Quarter Company - who reached the Maltings, utterly weary and footsore having covered the distance in 3 days, 12 hours - or upwards of 45 miles a day.

Within a day or so of our return we were Gunners!

The first home of 181 Field Regt R.A. was in and around Melton Mowbray in Leicestershire, and if we had trained hard in the K.S.L.I. we certainly trained doubly hard now - with fewer guards and patrols to find. Our first Regimental Commander was Lieut. Col. Herbert, D.S.O., O.B.E., and here was a man who believed most firmly in the saying that hard work kills no man, and he himself worked harder than anyone in his efforts to turn his Infantrymen into first class Gunners. I spent rather more than six months as his I.O. (Intelligence Officer), and more often than not it was the wrong side of midnight before I left the Office, but before many weeks were past it was evident that his policy was proving highly successful. All the Infantry Officers were sent away on special Gunner courses - the Captains to Larkhill and the Subalterns to the 123 O.C.T.U. at Catterick, where our second spell at O.C.T.U. was really most enjoyable as there was this time no threat of R.T.U. (Return To Unit) hanging over our heads. P.T. every morning at 07.00 hrs and exercises which took us all over the wilder hills of Yorkshire did everyone a power of good, while many of us enjoyed at least one game of soccer and two games of rugger per week - so that we were in good fettle by the time we returned to Leicestershire.

Our next move took us to Northumberland, and it was here that we first made the acquaintance of the Jocks of the 15th. (Scottish) Division with whom we were to fight. Grand fellows they were, and we did a great deal of training with them - Batteries training with their own Infantry Battalions - and Officers meeting in the evenings for further training in wireless etc, followed by most enjoyable parties in either their or our mess, so that soon we got to know and understand each other about as well as was humanly possible, and many of the friendships made in those days will last as long as life itself.

Shooting now took up most of our time, and we often expended more ammunition in a day's firing than peace time Regiments were allowed to fire in years - but gradually the Infantrymen became Gunners who felt that they could hold their own with the best in the land, and who had, in addition a thorough knowledge of Infantry training and tactics.

Inevitably, during this period drafts cost us many of our best and oldest friends, and eventually, too, we lost our Colonel, who took 132 Field Regiment to North Africa. He was more than sorry to have to give up a job which was but half completed, but the work which he had done for the Unit had laid sure foundations, and Lieut.Col A.C.E. Devereux, RA., found, when he came to us, a Regiment which was now proud both of its connection with the K.S.L.I. and of its progress in the Gunner World.

Month followed month, while the Regiment moved to Berwick-on-Tweed, Bardon Mill and Harrogate, and all the time training went on, with the exercises in which we took part growing ever bigger and of longer duration, while talk up and down the country as to the coming of "D" Day pointed to the fact that soon our years of effort would be put to the test.

Then, one day following a move to Thirsk, where the Regiment stayed for only a few weeks, we entrained for an unknown destination, and the following morning found us running into Worthing, where we were to put the finishing touches on Training and waterproof all our many vehicles preparatory to the adventures which everyone knew must lie ahead.

Some of our K.S.L.I. members had left us for one reason or another, among them Capt. J.L. Martin and Capt. J.S. Shields, both of whom we were to see next in Brussels, but there were still enough Shropshiremen left to remember that the fine record of the 6 K.S.L.I. in the 1914-18 war must be maintained in the World War at all costs. The Officers remaining with us who had actually served with the 6 K.S.L.I. were the following: Capt. R.G. Bristow; Captain A.D.G. Shaw; Captain N.W. Prutton; Lieuts J. MacOwan, T.J. Stokes and M.J.A. Walters, and, of course, myself. In addition we were fortunate enough to have upwards of 400 other ranks from the original 6th., and no one could possibly have wished for a finer batch of men to take to war.

Every day we expected to hear that "IT" had happened, and then one morning we discovered that the Commandoes, with whom we shared the billets and the hospitality of Worthing, had vanished in the night, and every man was on his toes. News came of the landing in Normandy, and in a couple of days we found ourselves in an embarkation camp outside London waiting for the word "Go".

In spite of all the training we had undergone in the backing of vehicles onto L.C.I's we embarked on Liberty ships, and the crossing, enlivened by a Troops' impromptu concert, was uneventful. Dawn of the 15th. June 1944 found us off the Normandy coast at Arromanches - and what a sight awaited our eyes as the dawn broke. On every side was to be seen the might of the Navy, for the surface of the sea was dotted, as far as the eye could see, with every kind and type of Naval Craft. Close to shore L.C.I.'s barges and other, weird looking craft were making their way from Liberty ships to the beach loaded with men, guns, vehicles equipment, and then returning for second and following loads; nearer the Liberty Ships long low grey destroyers were on guard watching and waiting for any Hun aircraft that might dare to attack the great Armada in daylight, while out at sea the great Capital Ships pointed their enormous guns at the forlorn looking smoking beaches.

Bill Busby - A personal account

Bill Busby wrote to me from his home on the Isle of Wight, with his memories of the time he spent with 6 KSLI:

I joined the Bn in the first week of January 1941 and went to a place called Wainfleet, just south of Skegness. A coy. commander named Martin was there but I did not stay with him for very long - spent most of my time with the farmer who owned the place and went duck shooting with him almost every evening along the coast within the area where the platoons were living in the trenches. It was a pretty bitter winter but having met the CO. Basil Munn, I was transferred to HQ coy with Ivor Reeves as coy. commander. I was given command of the carrier platoon as well as the mortars because I had already done a mortar course, apart from the fact that no one else knew anything about them. It was a very interesting time and having known Ivor for some years, we got on very well together. I was more or less my own boss and travelled all over the area covering the line from Mablethorpe down to Skeg. The Bn HQ moved from place to place but was never very long anywhere. Whilst in Spilsby we had the big pub where most of the HQ people lived, and that was where I first met John Meredith. He replaced another Meredith who, I think was the organist at Singapore Cathedral. Basil was a stickler for church parades and we all had to attend. Although we were looking forward to having a crack at the Germans we never saw them, but it was here that a German bomber dropped his load on the way home and they landed just up the road on a garage. Basil's brother was 2i/c and he decided to get under the dining table for cover. It was here that Basil told his brother to leave the next day. Basil and I went to see what damage had been done and we did our best to try and clear up the mess. there was little we could do except look for bombs which had not gone off, we searched carefully, found nothing, but my carriers were close by and I had to move them. You will know the carrier Pl. Sgt, was it Bourne? He was a damned good chap. Incidentally, Bill Munn did leave us the next day! Over this period Basil decided that every man in the Bn should learn to throw a 36 grenade and I was the only bloke who knew anything about them, so I was the joe egg who had to travel up and down to each platoon, and one by one each soldier got into a trench with me to throw a grenade. there was a snag because so many of the grenades failed to go off, and I found that they were not being cleaned properly as they came coated in grease. On one day alone I had to go on to the sand below no less than 19 times. I got Sgt Rooke with glasses to watch the grenade in case the striker went down. Only one ever did and it was just as I was about to pick it up, when down went the striker. I ran three paces and dived to the ground with my feet towards the bomb. It was a bit frightening I finished up with my trousers having a great rip across my bottom, no real injury. There were times when the bomb was sitting on top of the sand, so I could have a shot at it with a 303, otherwise I always carried a lever and pin to put in the thing. After this I made sure that all the grenades were cleaned properly. I suppose it frayed my nerves a bit although I never worried about it at the time. Another episode, when some one from Northern Command invented the 76 Grenade. I was sent three, I had never seen such things, no instructions on how to use them but they had a tape around them and looked just like a thermos flask. I phoned Northern command and they sent a despatch rider with a letter to say how many went in a box and the type of explosive! No help at all, so I had to do a bit of guess work. Basil arranged for the whole Bn to march to a central point between Skeg and Mablethorpe where I was to give a demo on how to throw the things. I selected a place in the bluffs in the middle of John Shields Company area. John and I decided to dig two trenches, one behind the other and I would throw the grenade from the forward one in the bluffs whilst John would be in the rear, with a shovel ready to dig me out in case I blew myself up. I simply had to throw the things over the triple dannert on to the sand below, it all sounds very simple but when I threw the first one over the wire, nothing happened. Then I was obliged to get through the wire and pick the bloody thing up! I was a bit terrified at the time, and all the Bn had to march back to their trenches up and down the line, what a lark it was. At the time I was living, in a newish hotel near Ingoldmells, sharing a room with Teddy Corbett, we had a guest night that evening the Brigadier was coming. Anyway going upstairs for a wash and brush up Teddy went across the corridor for a bath whilst I waited my turn. I had these bombs with me and I thought I'd take another look at them and decided to roll one along the floor. There was such a bang and it blew all the windows out of the front of the hotel. It also burnt up both the bed rolls which were lying on the bed. I was blinded for a few minutes but not hurt. It was reported to me that Basil who was in the bar with the Brigadier said " You can guarantee that was Busby". Quite frankly I never did find out how it happened, but it cost me £19 for new windows, what a fool I was in those days. It was about the same time that the sticky bomb was introduced and I had to go along to the demo, I also tried one out, it actually worked, not that I ever had to use one. I wandered around the countryside with carriers and a couple of motorcycles, one of the motorcyclists was a star of dirt-track racing and he gave us all sorts of demos. Unfortunately during one week I had three crashes with motor cycles, ruining them and the Brigadier gave orders that I was not to be allowed to use them. The whole army was tight on vehicles in those days. We had a CSM Coombes who took a PU without permission, he was given a district court martial and reduced to the ranks, an ex 2nd Bn man, 4030999 was his number. During this time, Basil told me one day to " to put another pip on my shoulder" later on in the day he asked me where it was, and I told him it wasn't the sort of thing I carried around with me! Never the less that was the day I was made up to Captain. I was instructed by Ivor Reeves to teach everyone I could get hold of to drive a Bren Carrier and one day I got hold of some mess servants, including the lance corporal who ran our mess in a semi-detached house we had taken over. Off we went for a ride along a road at the back of Butlins holiday camp. The lance corporal was driving and I was standing in the front of the carrier giving him instructions. We arrived at a canal called 40ft canal, there was no paving but a grass verge a couple of feet wide running alongside, the driver got one track on the grass verge and it gradually started to run into the canal where it ended upside down in the water. There was only about three or four inches of the bottom of the carrier above the water. I realised that the driver was trapped and I dived under the water to try and help him out, I pulled his hair out but could not free him because his feet were trapped and although I pulled and pulled he eventually died in my arms. I then discovered one of the other chaps was also trapped by his feet but his head was just above the water, I held him up, just, at the same time doing my best to get his feet from under the carrier, but had no luck so I spent about an hour holding his head above the water, meanwhile the other two blokes got up the bank and ran for help, It was winter and freezing. Sometime later a Dutchman, a sailor from Royal Arthur (Butlins) came along and saw my plight, I'm blowed if he didn't jump from the bank onto the bottom of the carrier which really put the wind up me because the carrier went down deeper in the water, so the poor chap whose head I was holding went under! I bawled at him to get off. Over the next hour I was treading water until eventually a couple of my carriers came along attached a couple of wire ropes and hauled us out which enabled us to release the trapped man. We were both taken to hospital and thawed out, the poor lance corporal was a married man with two children. It was a terrible experience and very upsetting, but I remember Basil or Ivor saying to me "If you can teach 100 men to drive these bloody things and only lose one, you will be doing well" This was all reported in the local paper and I'm pleased to say I never lost anyone else. I kept away from all the bigger dykes and canals although they were everywhere. As you know I left the battalion in November 1941 when I was posted the 3rd Gurkha Rifles where I served three years on the North - West Frontier.

Three unknown soldiers relax in dugouts between fighting.
Guns ready for action in the background. Note rifle stack on right.

FOP near Ueltzen April 1945, F/Ground, Sgt Telfer (6KOSB)
B/Ground, Gnrs Mountford, Jenks. Note Sgt Telfers Sten Gun.

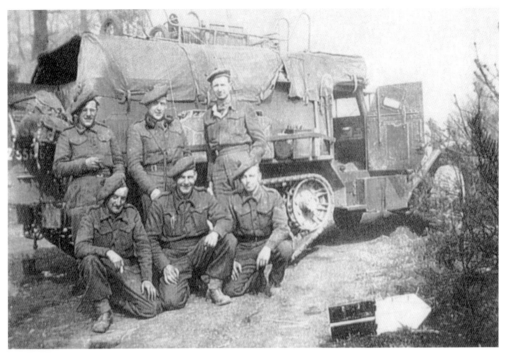

Fop Team 177 Bty April 1945, Rear: Gnrs Hogg, Goddard, Major Browne
Front: Gnrs Richardson, Ballymont, Sgt Jennings.

CP Team 177 Bty Nr Artlingen, L/R Capt Stokes, L/Bdr Watts, Gnrs Holmes, Vincash
(with sten gun) Jones, Palmer, Hambleton, Richardson. Ready for grub!

Digging Gun Pits, L/R BSM Oliver, U/K, Sgt Layton, Lt Mitchell, L/Bdr Newall, U/K.
Just outside Vynen - Vynen church steeple in the background.

In action! - 178 Bty. East bank of the Rhine 25th March 1945.

L/Bdr. Howarth   L/Bdr. Westwood   L/Bdr. Winkle

L/Bdr. Dodd   Unknown L/Sgt.   L/Cpl. Freddie Poole

Lt. David 'Sam' Small   Lt. Wladyslaw Rolski Polish Interpreter   Lt. Angus McLeod

Bdr. 'Pinkie' Fisher

Lt. DFA Trewby

Capt. George Easter

Capt. Moss Walters

Capt. Nigel Prutton

Capt. Ray Bristowe

Unknown

Brig. E.O. Herbert & Gen.Omar Bradley

Capt. A.J.J. Cory-Wright

Unknown Bdr.

Bdr. Jones

Bdr. Brooker

Bdr. George Aspley MM

Bdr. Griffin

Bdr. H. (Ginger) Forknall

Bdr. Moore

Unknown Bdr.

Unknown Gnr.

Gnr. Cartwright

Gnr-Dvr. Handby

Gnr-Sig. Horton

Gnr. Wain

Gnr. Jervis

Gnr. Rees

Gnr. Walker 21

Gnr. Walker 48

Gnr-Dvr. Canta   Gnr-Dvr. Harold   Gnr-Dvr. MacDonald

Gnr-Dvr. Wakely   Gnr-Sig. Harding   Gnr. Harris

Gnr. Sam Hassal   Unknown Gnr.   Gnr. Timmins

Lt. Ron Foulds

Maj. John Robertson

Rose

Sgt. E. Mottram

Sgt. E.W. (Ted) Packer

Sgt. Fred Darby

Sgt. George Cowern

Gnr. George Neal C Troop   Gnr. Frank Foster D Troop

Officers Mess 178 Bty Breitenfelde 1945,
Rear: 2/Lt Rwiatowski, Lt Foulds, Lt McLeod, Lt Mitchell, Lt Gow, Capt Ducquenoy.
Front: Capt Meredith MC, Capt Sharpe, Maj Grahame, Capt Shaw DSO, Capt Trewby.

Handing in the guns. Rear: Gnr Johann, L/Bdr Warmington, Bdr Green, BSM Clacker,
Gnr Broadhead, Gnr Hickman, Lt Hewitt. Row 3: Gnr Dock, Sgt Bull, Gnr Wilson,
Bdr. Onions, Gnr Stokes, Gnr Dimmock, Gnr Beddow, L/Bdr Milner, Bdr Bugler.
Row 2: Gnr Roberts, Gnr Bordwell, Gnr Tweedle, Bdr Hamilton, Gnr Fitzmaurice,
Gnr Kensey, Gnr Baker, Lt Wright. Front Row: Bdr Crouch, Gnr Berwick, Capt Stokes,
Gnr Jennings, Gnr Turney, L/Bdr Houlgrave.

Lt. Cornes and Sgt. Shelby with 25pdr complete with gun platform.

Gnr. Albert Smith (left) and Gnr. Parsons. An excellent rear shot of the 25pdr.

Sgts Mess 178 Bty Molln 1945, Featuring, Sgts Fletcher,
Chivers, Mottram, L/Sgt. Eden and BQMS Norcross.

Luneberg 27th April 1945. L/R Maj Gen Barber GOC 15(S) Div, Lt Gen Barker GOC 8 Corps,
Brig Bolton CRA 15(S) Div, Brig Colville C/O 227 Bde. (Courtesy I.W.M.)

Vehicles ready for the final push.

Guns also ready for the final push.

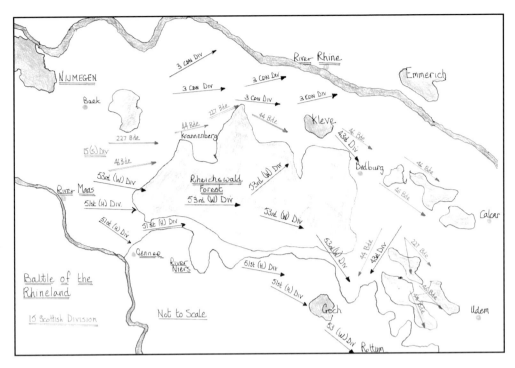

Battle of the Rhineland - 15th Scottish Division.

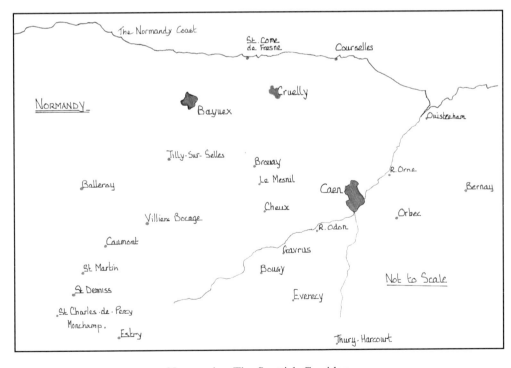

Normandy - The Scottish Corridor.

XXX

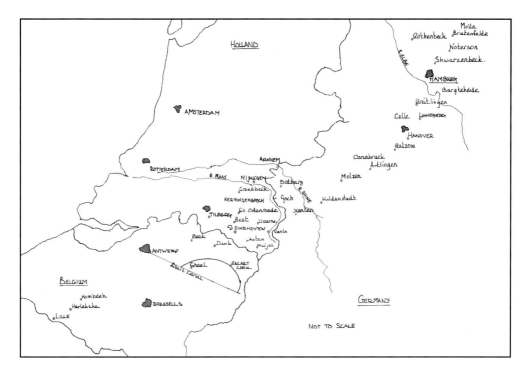

North West Europe - Advance to Germany.

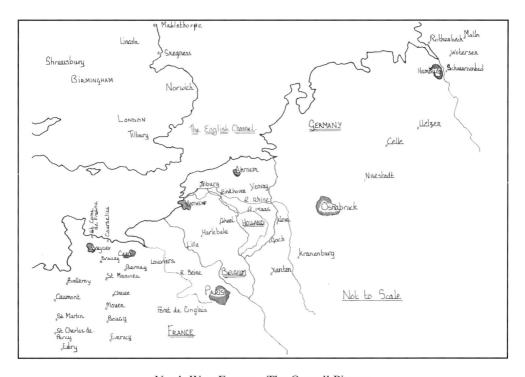

North-West Europe - The Overall Picture.

XXXI

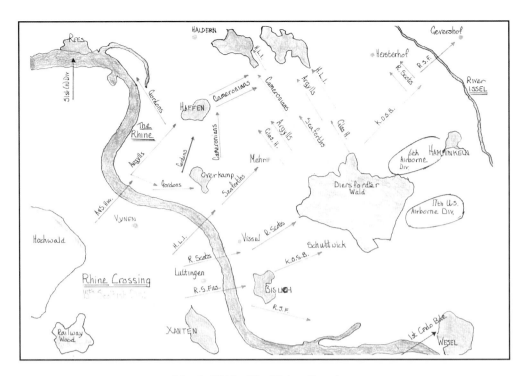

March 1945 - The Rhine Crossing.

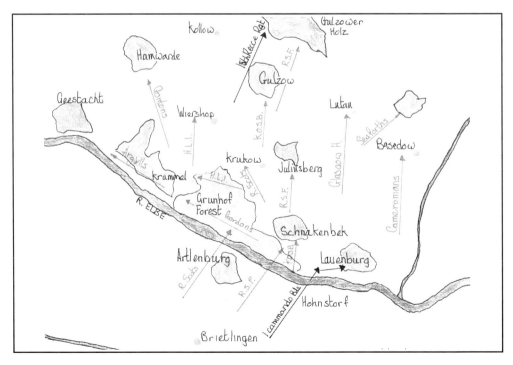

April 1945 - The Elbe Crossing.

Fred Parsons - A personal account

Fred Parsons was A Bdr / Ack Signaller /specialist with D Troop 178 Bty. His story was written during the fighting and was not completed. This account was for inclusion in the Divisional magazine the 'Tam O'Shanter'.

The Division returns

Yesterday the series of articles on the exploits of the Division in the last war which have been published in the 'Tam O'Shanter' from time to time, came to an end. The last words were; "but they established a tradition of courage steadfastness, and loyalty. We of the 15th Scottish, in this war have not let them down." The time will come in the not far distant future, when we shall be able to sit down and view in retrospect the magnificent achievements of the Division which have carried on the tradition, and a history will be written so that these achievements may be recorded for posterity. It is fitting that, in the hundredth edition of the Divisional news sheet, we should sketch in broad outline, the events that will form the basis of the major part of the history when it comes to be written.

Battle of the Scottish Corridor

Our long period of waiting at home when we preparing to play our part in the greatest invasion campaigns of all times, came to an end in June 1944, and shortly after D-Day we landed on the Normandy beaches. Our first action, which has become famed as "The Battle of The Scottish Corridor" during which such names as Coleville, Granville, Mouen, and Cheux came to the fore, commenced at 0730 hrs on the 26th June. Our attacks drove a wedge into the enemy lines, and enabled us to gain the vital Odon crossings. It earned the commendation of Field Marshal Montgomery and General Dempsey and established our reputation in the invading armies.

Everecy

On 15th July we were again committed, this time on the Everecy sector and battles were fought around Esquay, Mondrainville, and Everecy itself. Here, our attacks drew off a great deal of the German strength and materially advanced the fall of Caen.

Attack from Caumont

By now, the American break-through was beginning to show itself, and on 23rd July we were moved over secretly to Caumont to play an important part in the plan. A week later the Division, for the third time, was used as the spearhead of the attack and, on 30th July, we pushed through to Sept Vents and Lutain, Hervieux and Les Loges, and by evening we were on Hill 309, our objective near St. Martin des Besaces. The C.in C. saw the Divisional Commander after the Battle. The sense of his comments was; "You broke right through the enemy defences without regard to the situation on your flanks. It is what defeats the enemy and opens the way for the breakout by Armoured Divisions." In a special order of the day the Army Commander wrote: "It was the 15th Scottish Div. Which broke through the enemy's main defence line…. You have set the very highest standard since the day you landed in France and I hope you are as proud of your achievements as I am to have you under my command." The Corps Commander added: " Your capture of the high ground in the area of the Bois du Homme was vital to the success of the whole Second Army plan." The following days saw grim struggles in the wake of the armour, in the Au Lounee, La caverie and Estry area. This ended when we were moved back to the Caen sector to stand by for the Falaise push, but events moved with such speed that we were not seriously committed as the pocket was closing. We left our parent Corps to take part in the appropriately titled "Operation Gallop". The Corps Commander wrote in a special order of the day, dated 12th August 1944: "There is no formation with a finer fighting spirit and finer record than yours".

Operation Gallop

The dash through France commenced; liberating village after village, we pressed on towards the Seine, and on the first day covered 30 miles. On the day after we reached our first objectives, Louviers, where we found the F.F.I. in control. We pushed on to the Seine and crossed the river. By the end of August we were mopping up in the Senneville – Le Thuits loop, on the other side, and had liberated Les Landelup. We continued through France and Belgium over the Battle Fields of the last War, through villages where the 15th Scottish had before won imperishable glory in battles against the Germans. Fittingly about this time the Divisional Commander received a note from one who, as he said " had the honour and privilege of serving with the Division in France in 1916/1917", expressing pride in the Division, which was adding to its great reputation of old.

Gheel

On 8th September we were mopping up roughly on the circumference of a semi-circle running east from Rouliers to Ghent, but it was not until we reached the Meuse – Escaut canal a few days later, that we were seriously halted. Against very stiff resistance we fought for the Gheel bridgehead, and drew off German strength while the main bridgehead on the canal was being made solid for the advance into Holland.

Into Holland

On 20th September we marched into Holland in the wake of the Air-Borne Troops, and, on 24th September were fighting on the Wilhelmina Canal. Fierce battles followed between Best and Schijndel, and the areas around such villages as Vluet, Hoefke, Olland, Donderdonk and St Oedenrode were bitterly contested'. This grim slogging match lasted until early October, when we were withdrawn to rest. On 19th October we began to return to the same sector, but this time it was for a break-through which culminated in the liberation of Tilburg. Our stay in Tilburg was all too short and on the 28th October we were ordered back to the east, to counter a German thrust from the Venlo area which looked like developing into a serious threat. As I write the Division is engaged in this sector, and is accomplishing the job for which it was brought over with the courage and efficiency it has shown in all its previous engagements. It is adding yet another page to its illustrious record of achievements.

Unknown - A personal account

The following article was found among the papers of 44 Brigade HQ at the Public Record Office, Kew (WO 177/4366). Despite enquiries via the Old Comrades Association I have been unable to find out who the Author was. It was most likely someone from HQ, the Bde Major or maybe the Intelligence Officer. Perhaps in the ensuing months I will find out. The account opens with a tribute to the Brigades supporting units, including a special mention in particular of their 'peerless Gunners'. The men of My Dads Regiment, 181 Field Regt.RA.

This short account is dedicated with grateful thanks to the Officers and men of the Royal Tank Regiment, The Royal Artillery, The Royal Engineers, The Royal Army medical Corps and The Middlesex regiment who supported the Lowland Brigade so efficiently in this battle. And especially is this tribute offered to the peerless Gunners of the Field Regiment affiliated to the Brigade, whose magnificent support has made this and every other success possible.

The Lowland regiments of the 15th (Scottish) Division have just achieved their greatest triumph in the crossing of the Rhine. These Battalions have had tremendous success and hard fighting since D-Day, in the bloody fighting on the River Odon, the great Caumont breakout, the crossing of the Seine, the desperate struggle in the Gheel Bridgehead, the brilliant capture of Tilburg, the smashing of the German counter thrust at Meijel, The "model operation" at Blerick, and lately in the smashing of the Siegfried Line and the storming of Cleve and Goch. Their achievements and reputation are second to none in 21 Army Group, and it was fitting that they were selected as 'opening batsmen' for the greatest operation of all – the crossing of the Rhine.

For this hazardous operation, the position of honour in the centre was given to the 15th (Scottish) Division. The Lowland Regiments were to cross at Bislich, just north of Wesel, secure a bridgehead and push on to link up with the airborne landings 5 miles beyond the river. At two-thirty on the morning of 24th March, The Royal Scots Fusiliers on the right and the Royal Scots on the left crossed the river in *Buffaloes** manned by men of the Royal tank regiment. The ground was extremely open and commanded by a high bank or bund 400 yds east of the river, on which the Germans had strong machine gun positions with wire and mines. These had been largely neutralised by our opening barrage, and the Lowlanders stormed up the bank with terrific dash and gained the ridge. The Royal Scots Fusiliers on the right ran into some Shumines, which caused casualties, but all the obstacles were overcome, and by four o'clock all Battalion objectives had been gained, with the capture of over 200 prisoners.

At four o'clock the King's Own Scottish Borderers went over in storm boats, formed up on the far side and entered Bislich. Fighting was hard, many knots of Germans resisting fiercely in the cellars and gardens, and Bislich was not finally cleared until about nine o'clock. After mopping up, the Battalions began pushing out to expand the bridgehead. At ten o'clock the air armada appeared overhead and dropped the Parachutists and gliders five miles ahead of the Lowlanders, with large numbers of Germans between the two forces. It was vital to link up and open a road to bring supplies to the Airborne Divisions.

At this point, the Lowlanders began to get the upper hand of the German defenders. The three Battalions carved through the opposition, and at two o'clock the historic link up took place between The King's Own Scottish Borderers and the 17th U.S. Airborne Division, five miles from the Rhine. At 4pm. The Royal Scots linked up with 6th British Airborne Division.

The day ended triumphantly. The Lowlanders had stormed the Rhine captured a thousand enemy prisoners and many guns, relieved the airborne Troops and opened the way up for the breakthrough. They were in tremendous spirits.

By morning a bridge was over the river and guns, tanks and vehicles were being ferried over. For the second time the lowlanders were ordered to secure a bridge over the river Issel, ten miles east of the Rhine. The Brigade set off at first light, and after overcoming fierce resistance by the enemy, they were well into the rear areas of the German 7th Parachute Division, which was still fighting north of Bislich. It was planned to capture the bridge that night as the King's Own Scottish Borderers pressed on. They were halted some four hundred yards short of the bridge by a heavy enemy counter attack by fresh Troops. For some hours there was a desperate hand to hand struggle which ended with the Borderers still on the ground, with 130 prisoners and 98 enemy dead around them.

At this point it was discovered that the bridge had been blown, and instead of being just a trickle the Issel was a fair size river some 40ft wide, there was nothing else for it but a frontal assault. At four o'clock, The Royal Scots Fusiliers launched their attack storming through the river, waist deep in water, in broad daylight against heavy machine gun and artillery fire. There can have been few more gallant actions in the history of this famous Regiment, the dash and fury of the Fusiliers was so terrific that within the hour they had three companies across the river, and by evening 360 prisoners 'in the bag'.

More drama was yet to come, a bridge had to be built over the river to get supporting arms to the Fusiliers to enable them to hold the bridgehead. A violent thunderstorm had reduced all tracks to the river to a quagmire preventing the heavy bridging lorries access. The only possible route was the main road north along the Issel, which was still in enemy hands. At midnight a patrol of the King's Own Scottish Borderers roared along the road in lorries with Machine Gunners mounted atop. They got through unscathed and by daylight the sappers working like demons, had completed the bridge and heavy anti-tank guns were rolling into position. It was a great feat of engineering.

During the following day the Germans counter-attacked with force despite this the Lowlanders hung and gave not an inch. The Armoured Divisions were pouring through the hole punched by the Lowlanders and the Airborne Divisions, and as night fell on the 27th March, the enemy were streaming back. 44th (Lowland) Bde had been fighting for four days with the enemy on three sides, and opened up a road and bridge vital to the breakthrough and held it against all opposition.

*Buffaloes - Amphibious Personnel Carrier

Harry Holder - A personal account

On 26th March 1944 The Division approached the River Issel. The bridge having been blown up by the retreating Germans, Brigadier Cumming-Bruce made a plan to force a crossing on foot. This was carried out by the 6th Bn Royal Scots Fusiliers 44 Bde 15th (S) Division In a daring frontal attack 6 RSF stormed into the water. And waded waist-deep across the river firing as they crossed at a very active enemy. Described in the history of 44 Brigade as *" This brilliant operation, which showed magnificent courage and skill must take its place among the very finest feats of this well tried battalion"*. This Dramatic and moving account was recorded and written down by Harry Holder in March 1992.

We crossed the Rhine at about 2am on the 24th March. This, for us was the 'big one' but it turned out not quite so costly as we had anticipated. We had some adventures of course, but none that we couldn't handle. Then at 10 o'clock that morning the glorious sight of hundreds of gliders and Dakotas coming over our positions to land several miles in front of us. The sky was full of parachutes and the horrible sight of gliders being hit by anti-aircraft fire and the lads inside tumbling to earth and certain death. It was like so many pepper pots being shaken, and sprinkling the contents willy-nilly over the earth. This sight will live with me forever.

Within a comparatively short time the German guns fell silent and an eerie silence fell across the battlefield. It was the kind of silence that could be felt and was so unusual that I felt uneasy. Soon we spotted what appeared to be a giant approaching our lines from where the Para's had dropped. A man of normal height accompanied him and the sight was so strange that none of us opened fire. Thank god we didn't, it was an American, mounted on the shoulders of a German soldier. It turned out that he was the pilot of a crashed Dakota and had broken both ankles in the crash. He had taken the two Germans prisoner and forced them to carry him to our lines. He asked us not to shoot them (as if we would) as they had saved his life.

As far as I remember we held our positions till the next day, and then began to advance. It became clear why the German guns had fell silent the previous day.

The Paratroopers, in some cases had dropped right on to the German gun positions and wiped them out. At one point we came across a group of Paratroopers who had obviously been disarmed, lined up and shot. They lay still and silent, their limbs distorted in their final agony. If we had encountered any Germans in the next hour or so I am sure we would not have taken any prisoners.

We pressed forward to the sound of the pipes as Colonel Mackenzie had ordered the pipers to play to let the Paratroopers know that help was on the way. Red Berets popped out of the ground and from various farms and cottages. You can imagine how pleased they were to see us so quickly after their drop. They all must have had the Arnhem 'cock-up' in their minds when 2nd Army failed to reach them.

I think our original objective was the bridge over the Issel, which the Air-Borne had not reached. The Royal Scots had tried but had encountered heavy opposition, but in any event the Germans had blown the bridge. The 6th Bn. Royal Scots Fusiliers were ordered to force the river crossing on foot. We were briefed that our objective was a wood on the far of the river, code named 'Elizabeth'. We were to be ferried by *Kangaroos** to our start line that was a ditch-lined road and we were to dismount, and form up in the ditch. Between the River Issel and us was open ground of between 100 and 200 yards, then the river, then more open ground before we reached 'Elizabeth'. As a humble section leader I had no idea of the overall situation so I can only recount the action from the part that A company played in the attack. We moved off in *kangaroos*, 8-platoon leading and my section were in the leading *kangaroo*. Just as we reached the start line my tank was hit and set on fire. I ordered the section out but had trouble with one of the lads who was trying to free the driver. The driver looked dead to me and I had to beat my comrade with my rifle butt to get him out of the *kangaroo*. We jumped straight into the ditch, which was full of Germans. Some were waving white flags and some were shooting. The ditch was soon cleared and Major D.M. Gray gave the order to attack. We were out of that ditch like a shot and went hell for leather for the river firing as we went. Major Gray led the charge from the front and was first to the river. I was right behind him, and I remember pausing to let him jump in first so I could see how deep it was. What a crazy thing to do when I had a lot more to worry about. Men were dropping all the time and we waded into the river (Which came up to my chest) over the other side, and out into the woods.

'Elizabeth' was, from my memory not too deep and we started to dig in immediately I went to the edge of the wood to watch for any counter-attack, but all I saw was a wounded German about 60 yards away shouting for help. From out of a farm building came a German soldier, (He wore a white apron and hat so he must have been a cook), I emptied my magazine at him and missed with every shot! He carried the wounded man away and somehow I felt glad that I'd missed him.

By now Major Gray had assessed the situation and I think there were only 27 of us left. We had lost our Signaller and his set so we were virtually cut off from Battalion. Ammunition was low and jerry was very active. Major Gray asked for two volunteers to take a message back and L/Cpl Mitchell and Fusilier Johnson volunteered. At this point it was clear that we were under fire from all three sides, because as the Major and I stood at the edge of the wood looking back to the river, the bullets were whizzing overhead and clipping foliage off the trees.

The two volunteers set off on different headings. L/Cpl Mitchell didn't get far before he went down and Fusilier Johnson went down soon after. Major Gray looked at me and said "There's nothing for it Holder, you'll have to have a go". I stripped off my small pack and my webbing, keeping only my rifle and my bandolier. I took several deep breaths and ran like hell for the river. I slid down the bank into the water and rested with my back to the bank, chest deep in the river, getting my breath back. I started to wade across the river but was immediately picked up by a *Spandau** who put a burst two or three feet in front of me, a small bend in the river prevented him from getting a bead on me. Every time I moved he had a go and I was just about to try swimming under water when the miracle happened! It started to rain and there was such a terrific downpour that visibility was reduced to about 20 yards. I was off like a scared rabbit through the river and over the field to where I thought we had started from. By now the storm was easing, but I had no idea where Battalion H.Q. was located. Visibility had improved and I was able to have a good look round and I set off across a field at a smart trot. Suddenly jerry put a *Stonk** down and several airbursts seemed to be aimed at me personally. I dived into a ditch right on top of three Germans who were sheltering from their own Artillery. They were more surprised than me so I was able to deal with the situation very quickly.

Up and running through the fields desperately searching for Battalion H.Q. I spotted a lone British soldier in a slit trench. I ran over to him hoping he knew where I could find B.H.Q. But he was the only survivor of his section and was either Royal Scots or K.O.S.B. He couldn't help and I couldn't persuade him to come with me. He insisted he had to stay even though he was on his own and didn't know where his comrades where. I've often wondered whether he survived but I don't suppose I'll ever know.

I did eventually find B.H.Q. and gave my message to Lt.Col. Mackenzie. He sent for the Royal Artillery Officer who asked me to point out our positions, together with the known German positions on the Arial photograph he produced. The boys told me afterwards that the Artillery had helped break up one or two counter attacks.

Whilst I was talking to Lt.Col. Mackenzie, who should turn up but Fusilier Johnson. He was amazed to see me because he didn't know that I had been sent out after him because we thought him dead. He too had taken cover from *Spandau* fire but L/Cpl Mitchell had been killed.

Lt.Col. Mackenzie did not send me back with a message but told me to get into a nearby barn and get some sleep. I made the return trip to A company at dawn and we remained in 'Elizabeth' until midnight when the Royal Welsh Fusiliers came through us.

I have written this account of the Bridgehead over the Issel almost 47 years to the day since it happened. It is one action that remains clear in my head after all these years. If I shut my eyes and think about it I can remember it as though it was yesterday. The memories of other actions are dulled and vague but not this one. I think the reason for this is that I was completely on my own, had to make my own decisions, was responsible for my own actions and just had to get through. I also had to do things I would like to forget but can't.

*Kangaroo - A tank, with its top removed used for carrying Troops.
*Spandau - A German heavy machine gun.
*Stonk - A heavy Artillery barrage.

Chapter 14

SOME PERSONALITIES OF
6 KSLI / 181 FIELD REGIMENT

ASHTON Charlie; L/Cpl/Bdr. Dvr/Mech: One of my earliest contacts. Joined the 6th Bn. in June 1940 at the Depot. Member of the Bren Carrier Platoon, posted to HQ. Troop 181 Field Regt. and was driver to most of the FOP. Officers.

ASPLEY MM. George ; Bdr. FOP.: Signaller C Troop 178 Bty. spent most the war in one of the most dangerous positions as Signaller with FOP. Officer's at the front. received the MM for his excellent work in the Gheel Bridgehead. ex - member 6th Bn. KSLI.

BOURNE Colin; Sgt.: Bren Carrier platoon 6 KSLI, posted to HQ. Troop 181 Field Regt. Later to E Troop 179 Bty. Well respected and liked by the men. After the war became a leading personality in the Carpet Industry, Kidderminster.

BRANNAN Cyril (snowy); Bdr/sig.: This very popular NCO. Signaller was loved by all the men, a great cartoonist, his cartoons were a daily feature alongside Daily Orders, also a great comedian, a star turn at concert parties. Joined the Royal Artillery as a young man. As a youngster boxed under the name of 'Kid Thomas' Recommended for MM, awarded C-in-C's Cert. for his good work.

BUSBY William 'Bill'; Captain: joined the KSLI as a boy soldier, and was posted to the 6th Bn. as Weapons Training Officer. Comes from a long line of Busby's who were members of the Regiment. Although only with 6th Bn. KSLI for 12 months he has good memories of his time with the Battalion. He went on to spend his war with the 3rd Gurkha Rifles. At the time of writing, living in happy retirement on the Isle of Wight.

BROWN WT RSM. Remembered affectionately as 'Long' brown on account of his great height. Joined the Regiment in 1919, served in the 1st and 2nd Bn's. Before becoming RSM. with 6th Bn. RSM. Brown did not transfer to the Artillery, instead served as WO1 in Palestine and Iraq. Died in 1964.

CORY-WRIGHT AJJ.; Captain: Posted to 181 Field Regt. 5th March 1942, from HQ. 54 Div. One of the first Artillery Officers to arrive. Was Assistant. Adjutant with Regt., for some time before being posted to 177 Bty. as B Troop Leader. The only Officer of the Regiment to be killed in action,- on the very first day 26/6/44.

DARBY Fred; Sgt.: Conscripted into the 6th Bn. was re-posted to 181st Field Regt. on conversion, later C Troop 178 Bty. Promoted Gun Sgt. he was No.1 on my Dad's gun for some time. A Greengrocer by trade, from Chesterton Staffs. He was badly wounded in Holland.

EDEN Ted; L/Sgt.: Ex- KSLI reposted to 181 Field Regt. although not a professional boxer he became 15th Division middleweight champion in 1943. well respected by his comrades for his cool head. A Butcher by trade, he kept C Troop well fed during the conflict. Lives in Brimfield, near Ludlow. In his 80's at the time of writing.

FLETCHER Richard 'Dick'; Sgt: An ex - Regular Soldier who re-enlisted at the outbreak of war, to help train the new 6th Bn. conscripts. Joined the Artillery 177 Bty., was re - posted to 178 Bty. when Sgt Gunn was killed. A real character, but well respected by the Officers and men. Dick came from Leominster.

GUNN Arthur; Sgt.: A Regular Soldier, Gunnery Training NCO. He was sent to France at the last minute, and sadly killed, the day before the Regiment came into action. My Dad trained with Arthur while in the UK.

LOWDON ARS.; Captain RAMC.: Not strictly a member of the 181st. but attached as the Medical Officer only 24 years old when he was killed recovering the body of his Orderly from a minefield.

LEWIS Percy Gnr; Dvr/Mech: A great pal of my Dad's, and mine too. Unlike my Dad, he enjoyed recounting his war service and was rightly proud of it. Driver to the FOP. Officers C Troop 178 Bty. and 'Tractor' unit Driver ex - KSLI. He kept in touch with many of his old army pals, and was a great source of names and addresses, when I first began my project. Sadly Percy never lived to read my work. A Hereford man, lived in Leominster.

MAY John 'Ginger'; Gnr: From near Maidstone Kent, where he still lives. John joined the Regiment in November 1943, along with about 20 other men from the Royal West Kents, volunteered because he was 'fed up with square bashing' - He served alongside my Dad whilst training in the UK., when they became good pals, although he was about ten years younger. John was badly wounded in Normandy, losing an arm the day before the Regiment came into action.

MEREDITH MC John; Captain: Enlisted as a private in the 6th KSLI and quickly rose through the ranks. Posted to 162 OCTU only 4 Months after joining. rejoined the Battalion in December as 2/Lt. Became C Troop Leader, 178 Bty. and eventually Bty. Comm. after hostilities. Described as a natural leader, by the men who served with him, he was awarded a Military Cross and mentioned in despatches for his bravery. He was released with the honorary rank of Major, and Continued his military service with a spell in the Territorials. Born in Brecon, he spent a happy retirement in Hay-On-Wye. Herefordshire.

MULHOLLAND Philip; Captain: From Kent, enlisted into the 11th Bn. Worcestershire Regt. and commissioned 2/Lt. 6th KSLI in Sept 1940. Served as Command Post Officer (CPO) and E Troop leader 179 Bty.

NEAL George; Gnr.: My Father; Described by those who served with him as 'quiet and unassuming' enjoyed his time in the Army, though never one to discuss the War. Enlisted in July 1940, served in W coy. 6th Bn. KSLI. and later in C Troop 178 Bty. His conduct was described as 'Exemplary' and his testimonial describes him as 'A good, honest, hardworking soldier'. served on the gun as layer (No3)

PARSONS Fred; Bdr. CPO.Ack.: One of my 'youngsters' Fred joined the 6th Bn. when only 18 years old. becoming L/cpl before transferring to the Artillery, where he was promoted to Bdr. Ack (assistants) were responsible for calculating distance, trajectory, and fuse settings, and worked in conjunction with CPO's. Fred was also the unofficial Battery Barber. Very modest about the important job he performed, still living in Leominster.

SHAW DSO, ADG. (Dudley); Captain: A real enthusiast and supporter of my project, and has become a dear friend over the years. Although both Octegenarians, he and his wife, Dorothy, attend the annual reunion of the KOSB. in Galashiels, Dudley joined the Queens Westminster Rifles before the outbreak of the War, and was commissioned into the 6th Bn. KSLI. in December 1940. He spent some time in i/c Intelligence Section. Elected to transfer to the Artillery, where he became a fine Gunner Officer, D Troop leader 178 Bty. Distinguished himself in battle and was awarded the DSO. and the French, Croix de Guerre. Left the Army an Honorary Major. Now living in the peace and quiet of the Hampshire countryside.

SMITH Bill; Gnr/Sig.: Joined the Regiment along with John May from the Royal West Kents, both live in Kent where they remain great pals. Sgt. Gunn always felt that the two of them were 'trouble' when together, so he kept them separated, this was lucky for Bill as he could well have been on the same gun as John when it was hit. Bill was Signaller at the FOP with Capt. 'Duke' Ducquenoy, 178 bty. He was seriously wounded in Dec 1944, and after recovering served the remainder of the war with REME.

SMALL David Lieutenant; Called up Oct. 1939 after registration. He joined 142 field Regt.(The Royal Devonshire Yeomanry). Commissioned in Nov. 1943 and posted to 185 Field Regt. 49th (West Riding) Div. Served as Troop leader and GPO (Gun Position Officer). Posted to 181 Field Regt. in Dec 1944,when 185 Field Regt was disbanded and became Troop leader and GPO (Gun Position Officer) with E Troop 179 Bty.

THOMLINSON JH. Lieutenant; Taken on strength 05/04/42. joined from 123 OCTU. Posted to 177 Bty. Served as assistant Adjutant in Harrogate. Posted to RHQ as Intelligence Officer. One of the party of men who took the MO into the minefield to collect the body of his Orderley. At the end of the War he was invited to join the staff of HQ. RA. 23rd Indian Div. Under his old C/O RWB. Bethell.

Capt. Philip Mulholland

Was a student at Reading University when he was called up in July 1940 into the 11th Bn. Worcestershire Regt. He was a member of the Officer Training Corps at School so was selected to go before an Officers Selection Board (W.O.S.B.) and eventually dispatched to an Officer Cadet training Unit, at Sandhurst Royal Military College for a 4 month course. Commissioned into the 6th Bn KSLI September 1941, he joined them at Skegness on the East Coast. Returned from a signals course to join the new Artillery Regiment in Melton Mowbray. He served the war as Assistant and later Command Post Officer 179 Battery. At the end of the war he was on his way to join a Regimental holding unit in Belgium to await a posting to South East Asia command (S.E.A.C.) however, the war in Japan finished and he joined the 6th Field Regt. RA and went to Palestine and Eygpt as part of the British 3rd Division.

His recollections of early military life were quite horrendous, and give an insight into the sort of conditions that many conscripted men were thrust into. The 11th Bn. Worcestershire Regt. was formed in a tented camp on Hereford Race Course, hundreds of men from mixed backgrounds most of them either side of twenty like himself, but many in their thirties and married, These men found it particularly hard to adapt. The food was plentiful but revolting To save queuing for meals some men (at breakfast for instance) would pile porridge, and fried egg, bacon and bread all onto the same plate, others would rejoin the queue for each course after first washing their plate in a bucket of tepid water. They had to learn to distinguish the many different bugle calls, which summoned them to get up, attend parades, queue for meals and put them to bed at night. The early morning call (reveille) would result in a rush for ablutions to stand in line for a wash and shave in cold water, return to the tent, stuff the bedroll and kit into a kit - bag which had been last nights pillow, and then rush to be the first in line for breakfast. His military drill and training began with broomsticks, only NCO's were issued with rifles, and it was many weeks before they were issued with full battledress and rifles, as summer turned to winter the camp became a quagmire and getting up for a wash and shave in cold water would test the hardest of men. All this for less than £15 per week. They eventually moved to a camp at Bedford where conditions improved. He recalls the intensive Artillery training and the crossing to France, the start of operation " Goodwood" being delayed due to the storm in the channel which left them with time on their hands and not much to do. Most of the local farms had been evacuated and the farm animals left unattended, the phrase 'liberated' became a much used expression and 'liberated' chickens and eggs soon found their way into Army kitchens to supplement army rations. 179 Battery supported the 6th Bn. Scots Fusiliers, 44th brigade, and he remembers vividly the tough fighting conditions the Infantry endured. At his command post during the battle for Normandy he was continually being informed of enemy counter attacks, and recalls a report that enemy tanks were about to break through the Infantry line. They were warned that they were would have to fire over open sights at point blank range, although these attacks never materialised the tension at the guns was considerable. during the ' rush for the Seine ' he was was sent to forward to recce a sight for the Battery to rest for the night, and encountered a French farmer and his wife, who offered their house and buildings. The Farmer then dug up a bottle wine and with tears streaming down his face they all toasted the allied leaders including De Gaulle, while his wife remained quite unmoved by the incident. Lt. Mulholland continued to serve with 179 Bty throughout the campaign, and says the Artillery contributed greatly to the success of the Division, no attack being launched without a devastating Artillery barrage. the Scottish Infantrymen often had to admire the courage of the German soldiers as they still stood to fight after such a pounding. Any slight movement of armour or vehicles also bought a hail of high explosive shells.

Capt. TJ Stokes

Born at the 'Arbour', Brilley, Hay on Wye near the Welsh border and raised in the area, Tom Stokes quickly made his mark at the local school, winning a scholarship and going on to a College education. After his education he began a distinguished professional career in opthalmics which had to be put on hold as the world grew near to war. Seeing it's inevitability prompted Tom to join the Territorials, and he became a member of the 5th Bn. North Staffs Regt. which was a searchlight Battery and came under command of the Royal Engineers. So began his military career as Sapper 1095276. He was no stranger to the ways of the military having served in the college OTC (Officer Training Corps) where he gained a War Office Certificate A. That summer of 1939 he attended camp with his unit to put into practice the hours of training in the use of searchlights and small arms.

After several moves around the country with his searchlight Battery including duty at Ironbridge, Shropshire, and Birmingham, he finally ended up in Nottinghamshire. Out in the countryside near a small village called Plumtree, he and his small band encountered the generosity of Mr. and Mrs. Edson of the 'Ramblers'. A fortuitous move, for Tom was destined to marry one of their four daughters, Majorie. Just before Christmas 1939 Tom volunteered for 'special duties' and in February 1940, his comparatively comfortable existence came to an end when he found himself on a train to Dover, where he was to help form a new Pioneer Battalion of the King's Own Royal Regt. This new Battalion made up of Signallers and other specialists was soon equipped and formed into four Companies and before long the newly-formed battalion was sent to join the BEF (British Expeditionary Force) in France, landing at Calais on the 27th April 1940. Shortly afterwards the Battalion was ordered forward into Belgium, where Tom was to embark on a train journey that he describes as the worst experience of his whole wartime service. Twenty eight men and their equipment crammed into a cattle truck that was locked and bolted from the outside! They finally reached their destination, to be faced by total chaos, told that they had travelled too far and were ordered to march back. After about 10 miles they received the order "All roads to the coast". These roads were by this time choked with French and Belgian refugees, including the remains of their battered armies. It wasn't long before the refugee column became the target of merciless German Stuka bombers which continuously bombed and strafed the refugees. On 29th May he found himself, along with thousands of other survivors of the BEF on the beaches of Dunkirk where he and his comrades were under continual attack from the German Luftwaffe whose frequent visits brought death and destruction. Eventually, after a wait of nearly 24 hours, he managed to board a boat for England.

After recovering from his ordeal and a short visit to Plumtree, he rejoined the remnants of the 7th Bn. KORR. on the south coast only to discover he had been posted 'missing presumed drowned'. After a couple of weeks of reorganisation they moved to Rhyl, in North Wales, where the Battalion was re-equipped, and Tom was promoted to Sgt.in one move! A short while later the Battalion moved to Northern Ireland to continue its Infantry training and whilst stationed here Tom decided to apply for a commission. Within three weeks he was on his way to Bulford Camp to join 162 OCTU. On completion, with a new army number 187117, he was commissioned 2/Lt. and being a Hereford man he decided to apply for an appointment with the Herefordshire Regiment or its parent corps the King's Shropshire Light Infantry which he joined in May 1941 as an Officer in the newly formed 6th Bn. Which was then employed on Home Defence on the east coast.

Tom was one of the eighteen KSLI Officers who elected to to transfer to the Royal Regiment of Artillery when the 6th Bn. converted on the 1st March 1942. After Artillery training he rejoined his old unit, newly reformed as the 181st Field Regt. RA. in its training area at Melton Mowbray in Leicestershire. There, for a while he was attached to HQ. Coy. as Assistant Adjutant to Capt. Cory - Wright who had recently joined the new Regiment from HQ. RA. 54 Div. They were both eventually posted to B Troop, 177 Bty. The Artillery training continued apace with plenty of cross - country running, route marches, football and rugby, which were regular features of CRA (Commander Royal Artillery) Brig. 'Bosun' Hilton's training programme.

During the fighting for the break- out from Normandy, on the 29th July 1944, Tom was wounded in the arm, and was soon on a ship bound for England to recover. While in the UK recuperating he began to put together an account of his adventures. This was kept up and completed after hostilities in Germany and and eventually printed and published in a limited edition entitled 'Return To Europe'. I'm pleased to say a surviving copy was presented to me by Mr. David Small who served as a Lieutenant with 179 Bty.

Tom rejoined the Regiment on 5th March 1945 in time for the assault on the Rhineland and continued the fight into Germany. In 1994 he had a second book published entitled ' A Life's Journey ' a story of his colourful and eventful life, including his wartime service. During my research it became apparent that Tom was entitled to a Territorial Efficiency Medal which had never been awarded. I'm pleased to say that this has been rectified, the medal being Gazetted on the 15th Sept 1998. Taking time to adjust to the peace and quiet of civilian life, he returned to his work in Opthalmics, where he was involved in no small part in the development of contact lenses. Now living in their adopted Bolton with his wife Marjorie, they are both keen and active members of St. Marys Church Deane. I paid them both a visit in April 1998 when I had the opportunity to thank him for all his help and encouragement during my research.

Maj. ADG Shaw DSO

I first wrote to Dudley Shaw in October 1996. He, having been tipped off by Tommy Stokes of my project, explained that like so many of his comrades his wartime service had been pushed to the far corners of his mind, and that events and sequences were quite vague. However, his interest had been re - kindled by the 50th Anniversary of D Day, in 1994. In an effort to stimulate his memories I sent him copy pages from the War Diaries. His enthusiasm came to life and after exchanging many letters and telephone conversations I had the opportunity to visit him at his home ' Oakapples ', in Hampshire. Since that time I have made a couple of visits and interviewed him at length about his time with both the 6th KSLI and the 181st Field Regt. His first hand knowledge and renewed recollection of both units has made him one of my most important contributors, providing a valuable and interesting personal experience.

Whilst studying the photographs he sent me I discovered that he also was entitled to a Territorial Efficiency Medal which had not been awarded . Unaware of this error for more than fifty years. He quickly set about applying for his missing medal, which was gazetted on 17th March 1998, the qualifying date? - 27th June 1945!

He was cajoled into joining the Territorials much against his parents wishes by a group of pals who persuaded him that it was 'dead cushy' and provided a glamourous uniform. Thus he found himself enlisted in to the King's Royal Rifle Corps, Army No. 6898234, and posted to the 2nd Bn. Queens Own Westminster Rifles on the 17th April 1939. Having gained experience as a Territorial he decided to apply for a commission, and on 20th September 1940 was posted to 168 Officer Cadet Training Unit (OCTU) in Farnborough, and was commissioned 2/Lt. personal No. P/164853 on 20th December 1940. His first choice of posting was, of course, back to the KRRC. or, any other Infantry Regiment, Just one day later he joined The King's Shropshire Light Infantry, and went for his Infantry training. A couple of weeks later he was posted to the 6th Bn. and joined them on the east coast were they were on coastal defence duties. He joined X Coy. and one of Dudley's more colourful, though tiresome jobs was running the Tote for the C/O. RBS Munn who kept a stable of about twenty Greyhounds (Regimental Mascots?) This entailed, organising meetings. finding suitable venues, and pacifying the local Constabulary in the event of 'incidents' involving rowdy Soldiers. Constantly harassed by the Betting and Licensing Board his Soldierly duties, in comparison were easy.

On 1st March 1942 when the Battalion was converted to the 181st Field Regt. One of his immediate tasks was to accompany the new C/O, Lt.Col. E.O. Herbert DSO to recce the area in Melton Mowbray were the new Regt. was to commence its Artillery training. This was a daunting task, as he explained, he was an Infantryman and had no idea of the requirements needed for an Artillery Unit. Anyhow he must have done a decent enough job for the area was deemed perfect. After a fairly uneventful 18 Months in Licolnshire he was one of the 18 KSLI Officers who elected to re - train and join the Royal Artillery. He was posted to Larkhill where he commenced an intensive Artillery Officers' course. During this time he was promoted to the rank of Lieutenant. on 21st June 1942, and re- posted to 181st on 1st August 1942. He rejoined his old unit in Melton Mowbray, much changed now. although the core of the Regt. were ex-KSLI personnel (484) there had been a huge draft of Artillery personnel, and they were starting to look like an Artillery Field Regt. He was originally posted to S Bty. Which was the Signaller and Specialist training Bty. Eventually becoming D Troop leader 178 Bty. after being promoted to Captain on 14th February 1943, and after the three Bty's had been re-designated 177/178/179 on 1st January 1943

His coolness and leadership under fire and in battle conditions were always to the fore, he received mentions in the Regt. War diary. The history of the 6th Bn. KOSB. the history of 15th(S) Div. and the history of 44 Bde. Command Post Bdr. Ack. Fred Parsons recalled an incident when they were under air attack being straffed *"We all dived under the nearest cover we could find, Dudley was running around waving his pistol about, screaming at us to get out and start firing at the B****."* With typical modesty he told me that he took each day as it came and thanked God that he survived it, mainly on wits and adrenalin. It was only as the Regiment fought its way into Germany that he started being cautious realising that the War was coming to an end.

His success with his men seems to have been an ability to assess their abilities and shortcomings and working with them. He told me a story about his Bdr.Ack at the FOP. His name was Bennall, excellent at his job, but inclined to nervousness under fire, Dudley discovered that trying to light a 'Tommy Cooker' under these conditions was almost impossible, as the confusion and blast invariably blew it out! This infuriated Bennall whose determination to get a brew up, took his mind off the danger of being killed! so when the shells started falling all around them Dudley would turn to Bennall and tell him *"come on Bennall lets have a cuppa!"*

His courage was recognised with two awards for distinguished service. By the French, after the Battle of Normandy with a Croix de Guerre, and later in February 1945 as the Division made its assault on the River Maas, he took command of the leading company of 6 KOSB, which had lost its Company Commander. Using his skill as an ex - Infantry Officer, during the next 48 hrs. he continued to organise and direct the Infantry Company to enable it to reach its objective, while at the same time giving instructions to his own Artillery Regt. bringing down destructive fire on the enemy. for this exceptional action he was awarded the DSO. one of only two to the Regiment. At the end of the War, in 1946, he was posted to 109 and 20 LAA. Regt. on the disbandment of the 181st Field Regt. He was granted the honorary rank of Major and released to the reserve on the 4th June 1946.

Maj. WM Busby

Bill Busby enlisted into the 2nd Bn. KSLI as a boy on 9th Jan 1929, after running away from a somewhat unhappy childhood. He was continuing a family tradition that was started by his Grandfather many years earlier, who was at his time Bandmaster of the 2nd Bn. Bills Father, who fought in both the South African War and the Great war also served with the 2nd Bn. He distinguished himself by becoming the Regiments first CSM. recipient of the Military Cross, he was also mentioned in despatches, and was so seriously wounded later on that he was rendered unfit for Military service. On his recovery he was to continue his Military career as an instructor to the St. Lawrence College OTC. where he continued to serve for another 24 years. Bills first posting was in the Band where most boy soldiers begin their careers. He learned to play th clarinet and his army number was 4030943. He became a private soldier on 29th Nov. 1932, on his 18th birthday, and was appointed L/cpl. in 1933. Serving at home in Aldershot, Colchester and Lichfield, he was posted to the Regimental Depot in 1936 and promoted to Cpl. in the same year. He continued his service in Shrewsbury, at the Depot and at Pembroke Dock, where he was appointed L/Sgt. In Jan 1939 he was posted overseas to serve in Bermuda, Curacao and Jamaica. In Nov 1941 he was commissioned as Lt. into the newly formed 6th Bn. KSLI. joining them on the east coast in Lincolnshire. As the Battalion was made up almost entirely of conscripts, Bill was appointed Weapons Training Officer and O/C. the Bren Gun Carrier platoon. Whilst serving in the 6th Bn. the C/O. Basil Munn ordered Bill *"to put another pip up"* much to his surprise, and it was in this manner that Bill was promoted to Captain.

On learning that that the 6th Bn. was to be converted to an Artillery Regt. and not wishing to become a Gunner, Bill joined a group of 25 volunteer Captains for service in the Middle East. At this point in November 1941 Bills service with 6 KSLI was bought to an end, and although not with them long, he remembers that the Battalion was a particularly friendly unit, and cannot recall any distasteful incidents during his time there.

He was eventually posted to the 3rd QAO. Gurkha Rifles, India on the North-West Frontier. During this period he was promoted to the rank of Major, and later commanded a jungle warfare training unit with which he served for 3 years. After the war ended Bill returned to the UK and the 2nd. Bn. in 1946. serving in Cyprus. On return to the UK. and after a short spell he was again posted abroad to serve as Weapons Training Officer to the Austrian Police force, becoming O/C. WTO. Head Quarters He was later transferred to the RWAFF. and saw service in the Gold Coast, Sierra Leone and Gambia. He lowered the Union Jack for the last time in the Gold Coast, but stayed on for an extra year in an advisory post. Returning once again to the UK. he was posted as Camp Commandant at Eastern Command in Hounslow until he was *"booted out"* (his words) in 1959 after 30 years service. After retiring from Military service he joined the staff of Barclays Bank where he served for 12 years before retiring to the Isle of Wight, where I visited him in 1998.

Maj. John Meredith MC (1912 - 1992)

Born and raised in Brecon, John Meredith was living and working in Whitchurch, Shropshire, on the staff of local National and Provincial bank, when he enlisted into the 6th Bn. KSLI on the 26th July 1940, and was given the number 4040591. His potential as a man with fine soldiering qualities was soon spotted by his superiors and on 26th Sept 1940, he took his first appointment a A/U/L/Cpl. By October of the same year, following quick promotion he attained the rank of Sgt. i/c No.9 platoon W coy. This was the same platoon in which my Father was serving. He was eventually put forward to attend the Officer Cadet Training Unit (OCTU) to earn a commission. On the 21st Nov.1940, only 4 months after enlisting he was reposted to the 6th Bn. as 2/Lt. serving in 15 platoon Y coy. Later that year, in December he was posted on a military small arms course to attend a 3" Mortar Course and on 1st Jan. 1941 was o/c Mortar Platoon.

When news came that the 6th Bn. was to be converted to an Artillery unit John was one of the eighteen KSLI Officers who decided that he would like to transfer. He attended the Artillery Officers training school at Catterick. After completing the course the Officers were reposted to their newly formed Field Artillery on 1st Sept. 1942. He continued to develop and trained in the field with the men who had already come to regard him with great respect. Promoted to Lieutenant on 15th Sept 1942 he was posted to Q Bty. which was the training Battery for the would be Gunners, and promoted to Captain on 1st Jan. 1943.

By the time of the invasion of France John was Leader C Troop 178 Bty. During the fierce fighting in Normandy and Holland, under the most difficult and trying conditions, his bravery, leadership and compassion, was to prove immeasurable, and his concern for his men was clear when I was invited by his son Bill, to study his fathers personal papers and momentoes, and found amongst them details and notes on all the men of his platoon and later his Troop. These included a personal letter to the next of kin of those in 178 Bty. that were killed in action. Percy Lewis and Charlie Ashton were both drivers for Capt. Meredith and spoke of their total confidence and respect for his judgement and authority, and his coolness and determination when under fire. Always at the front with the infantry as Forward Observation Officer (FOO). It was Charlie Ashton who was acting driver in the incident recorded in the History of the 15(S) Div. (p.70) on 16th July 1944, when, after temporarily losing his bearings and finding himself on the outskirts of an unknown village, Capt. Meredith called for a fire plan on a village called Everecy in order to regain his bearings. Almost immediately shells began falling all around them, They were actually in Everecy which was still in enemy hands! He ordered Charlie to turn the Carrier around smartly and beat a dignified retreat.

He continued to lead his men through France, Belgium, and Holland right into Germany, directing fire plans to support the infantry attacks or to destroy enemy armour and strongholds. The Division met fierce resistance in North Belgium where the advance was held up on the Albert and Escaut Canals. After continually directing fire for three to four days from a church spire which was constantly targeted by the enemy Capt. Meredith was wounded. Not until his duties were complete did he seek attention for his wounds. For this action, his bravery and dedication he was awarded the Military Cross. He returned to the Regiment for the assault on the Rhineland and was wounded a second time during the attack and crossing of the River Elbe. For continued distinguished service in the continuing battles he was Mentioned in Despatches, a second award for gallantry.

After the hostilities, while serving in Germany, he was promoted to the rank of Major and given command of the Battery. After the Regiment disbanded John was reposted to 71 LAA Regt. RA where he finished his service. His enthusiasm for military life continued and after retiring from the Army he enlisted in the Territorial Army and on 18th August 1947 seven years after joining the 6th Bn. KSLI he was commissioned as Captain into 639 Heavy Regt. RA (TA) attending an Officers Gunnery course on 25th July 1947.

Appendix 1

ABBREVIATIONS

O.R's	Other Ranks
Pte.	Private
Gnr.	Gunner
Dvr.	Driver
L/Cpl.	Lance corporal
L/Bdr.	Lance Bombardier
N.C.O.	Non Commissioned Officer
Cpl.	Corporal
Bdr.	Bombardier
Bdr.Ack	Bombardier Assistant (to officer)
Sgt.	Sergeant
W.O.	Warrant Officer
R.S.M.	Regimental Sergeant Major
B.S.M.	Battery Sergeant Major
B.Q.M.S.	Battery Quarter Master Sergeant
B/C.	Battery Commander
2/Lt.	2nd Lieutenant
Lt.	Lieutenant
Capt.	Captain
Maj.	Major
Adj.	Adjutant
G.O.C.	General Officer Commanding
C.O.	Commanding Officer
Coy.Com.	Company Commander
C.R.A.	Commander Royal Artillery
2i/c	2nd in Command
Brig.	Brigadier
Lt.Col.	Lieutenant Colonel
Lt.Gen.	Lieutenant General
A/Cap/ Lt / etc.	Acting / Captain etc.
T/Capt/ Lt / etc..	Temporary Captain etc.
W.S/ Capt / Lt / etc.	War Substantive Captain etc.
I/0.	Intelligence Officer
M.T.O.	Motor Transport Officer
W.T.O.	Weapons Training Officer
M.O.	Medical Officer / Messing Officer
Q.M.	Quarter Master
F.O.P.	Forward Observation Post
F.O.O.	Forward Observation Officer
C.P.	Command Post
C.P.O.	Command Post Officer

Div.	Division
(s) Div.	15th (Scottish) Division
Bde.	Brigade
Regt.	Regiment
Bn..	Battalion
Coy.	Company
Pl.	Platoon
Bty.	Battery
Tp.	Troop
Sec.	Section
Sub.Sec.	Sub-Section
H.Q.	Headquarters
R.H.Q.	Regimental Headquarters
B.H.Q.	Battalion Headquarters
Inf.	Infantry
Inf.Bde	Infantry Brigade
S.E.A.C.	South East Asia Command
R.A.	Royal Artillery
R.E.	Royal Engineers
R.S.	Royal Signals
R.A.M.C.	Royal Army Medical Corps
R.E.M.E.	Royal Electrical & Mechanical Engineers
R.A.O.C.	Royal Army Ordnance Corps
R.H.A.	Royal Horse Artillery
L.A.A.	Light Anti- Aircraft (Regt)
L.C.I.	Landing Craft Infantry
L.C.T.	Landing Craft Tank
H.E.	High Explosive
Anti -Tk	Anti-Tank
A.P.	Armour Piercing
K.I.A.	Killed in action
K.O.A.S.	Killed on active service
L.G.	London Gazette
S.D.	Service Dress (cap)
F.S.	Field Service (cap)
D.S.O.	Distinguished Service Order
M.C.	Military Cross
M.M.	Military Medal
D.F.C.	Distinguished Flying Cross
M.I.D.	Mention in Despatches
K.S.L.I.	King's Shropshire Light Infantry

44th Lowland Brigade

8 R.S.	8th Royal Scots
6 R.S.F.	6th Royal Scots Fusiliers
6 K.O.S.B.	6th King's Own Scottish Borderers

227th Highland Brigade

10 H.L.I.	10th Highland Light Infantry
2 G. H.	2nd Gordon Highlanders
2 A&S.H.	2nd Argyll & Sutherland Highlanders

46th Highland Brigade

9 Cams	9th Cameronians
2 GL. H.	2nd Glasgow Highlanders
7 S.H.	7th Seaforth Highlanders

Appendix 2

COMMANDING OFFICERS

6th Bn. KSLI/181 Field Regiment RA

MUNN Robert Basil Shepherd MC.(1918) Commissioned into the KSLI early in the Great War. Munn joined 2nd Bn. KSLI as a 2/Lt on first appointment, in the Ypres salient, at the end of May 1915. Promoted Lt. 1/10/1915, he was subsequently extra-regimentally employed with the Machine Gun Corps for the remainder of the War, and won an MC. as a Captain early in 1918. After the War he served with 1st Bn. KSLI in Bombay, 1921. Promoted Major, on the Reserve List of Officers, 7/9/1922. He was recalled to the colours on the outbreak of the Second World War. Appointed to command 6th Bn. KSLI. on formation, June 1940. T/Lt/Col. 4/10/1940. Munn remained CO. of the Battalion throughout its existence, and on conversion of the unit to RA. was re - posted to Infantry duties. At one time he had been employed as Director of Advertising for the BBC.

BETHELL Richard Brian Wyndham DS0.(1945) Born 1906. Educated at Tonbridge School and RMA. Woolwich. 2/Lt. RA. 1926. Served 1939-45, (France, Norway, Italy and ALFSEA.) T/Lt/Col. 31/8/1942: Lt.col. 1944. CO. 181 Field Regt 6/8/44 Brigadier 25/3/1954 ADC. to HM. the Queen 1957 - 59. retired 1959.

DEVEREUX Almeric Clifford Eustace MA. Born 1905. Educated, Westminster School and Selwyn College, Cambridge. 2/Lt. RA. (from General List TA) 1926. Served 1939 - 45 (France, 1939 - 40 and 1944). CO. 181 Field Regt. RA 6/8/1942: T.Lt.Col. 6/11/1942: Brigadier 7/4/1956. Commander Plymouth Garrison 1957 retired 1957. A graduate of the Staff College.

HERBERT Sir (Edwin) Otway KBE.(1955) CBE (1944) CB (1946) DSO (1940) and bar (1943) Born 1901 Educated Felsted and RMA woolwich 2/Lt. RA. 1921. Served in France 1939-40 and 1944-46 (mentioned in despatches four times), North Africa (First Army) 1942-43. T/Lt.Col. 17/2/1941. CO. 181 Field Regt 1/3/1942 Lt. Gen. 16/4/1954. GOC.in C. West African Command 1953 - 56. GOC. in C. Western Command 1957. Retired 1960. Colonel Commandant RA. 1956-66. High Sheriff of Anglesey 1964-65. Officer Legion of Merit (USA.) Knight Commander Order of Orange Nassau (Netherlands) Commander Order of Leopold II (Belgium). A keen sportsman, participating in most outdoor sports. Died 1984.

KEENE Thomas Patrick Born 1907 educated Marlborough College and RMA Woolwich 2/Lt. RA. 1927. Held certificate of the Gunnery Staff College (Field Branch) CO. 181 Field Regiment RA. 6/3/1945. A/Lt.Col. 19/4/1945: T/Lt.Col. 23/4/1945, Commandant Royal Pakistan Arty. School 7/4/55 -10/2/1957. Brigadier 27/8/1957. Retired 1960 Mentioned in Despatches LG. 8/11/1945.

Appendix 3

ROLL OF HONOUR 6TH BN. KSLI

Hanley Cemetery Stoke on Trent Staffs
Condliffe, Pte. John   4040395   3rd August 1940
Waterhouse, Pte. Ephraim   4040713   3rd August 1940
Hereford Cemetery
Bridgwater Pte. Walter Malpass   4040332   10th November 1940
Wenlock (Broseley) Cemetery
Venn L/Cpl. Henry   4040690   11th November 1940   (Age 29)
Witton Cemetery Birmingham
Rogers Pte.James Edward   4040057   11th July 1940
Ludford Church Cemetery
Meredith 2/Lt. Cecil Charles   126982   9th March 1941
St Mary's Churchyard Ross
Christopher Pte.Trevor Cecil   405954   29th October 1941
St Andrews Churchyard Shifnal
Powell Pte.Arthur   4040618   29th October 1941   (Age21)
Trelaw Cemetery Rhondda
Hicks Sgt.Charles Henry   4031218   13th February 1944   (Age 34)
Kandy War Cemetery Ceylon
Curtis Major Eric Colin   126979   8th September 1945
Doune Cemetery Girvan
McLean Dvr. William Allan   2382154   20th May 1944   (Age 21)
Royal Corps of Signals att. 6th Bn. KSLI

Appendix 4

ROLL OF HONOUR
181 FIELD REGT. ROYAL ARTILLERY

UNITED KINGDOM
Weston Beggard Churchyard
PRICE Gunner Mallwyn David 4040041 18th.Nov 1942 age 29, son of William and Mary Jane Price, husband of Florence Jane Price of Shucknall Hill.
Surbiton Cemetery
PACE Gunner Frank Reginald 11527621 8th May 1943 age 40, son of Frank Thomas and Edith Pace of St.Ives husband of Eileen Maude Pace of Tolworth.
West Bromwich Cemetery
WILLIS Gunner Sydney 4922849 18th May 1943.
Mountain Ash (Maes yr Arian) Cemetery
TEDSTONE Gunner Sydney John 4927108 19th May 1943, age 20, son of John and Eleanor Tedstone of Mountain Ash.
Largs
LYALL Lt. Donald Bourbon 273213 2nd Nov 1943, age 20 son of Robert Henry and Jessie Lyall.
McLEAN Gunner/Driver 2382154 killed in a motor cycle accident. no details 23rd May 1943
Ludlow New Cemetery
EDWARDS Gunner George Thomas Leonard 4039948 7th August 1944 age 30 son of George and Agnes Edwards of Ludlow.

FRANCE
Brouay War Cemetery
GUNN Sgt Arthur Ernest 750081 25th June 1944 age 38, son of William and Emily Gunn Husband of Kathleen Gunn of Lingfield Surrey.
McMORLAND Gunner Ralph 1790965 25th June 1944 age 22 son of Andrew and Jessie McMorland of Drongan, Ayrshire.
WHEATON Gunner Stanley 11002878 25th June 1944 age 35 son of Walter and Gertrude Wheaton of Bristol, husband of Rosina of Hanham.
Tilly sur Seulles War Cemetery
CORY-WRIGHT Captain Anthony John Julian 72690 26th June 1944 age 27 son of Geoffrey and Felicity Cory-Wright, husband of Susan Esterel of Catfield
Ryes War Cemetery
POUTNEY L/Bdr. Richard Henry 4040601 17th July 1944 age 32 son of William and Alice Poutney, husband of Regina of Wolverhampton.
St Manvieu War Cemetery
WOOLEY L/Bdr. Idris 4040092 29th. June 1944 age 24 son of Idris and Caroline Wooley of Sparkhill Birmingham.
CORDELL Bdr.Victor Raymond 4039928 1st July 1944 age 33 son of Frank and Henrietta Cordell Husband of Edith Cavell Cordell.
MELLOR Gunner Cyril 1078279 20th July 1944 age 34 son of Henry and Sarah Husband of Margaret Mellor of Manchester.

Bayeux War Cemetery
TYRELL Gunner John Allanson 1148922 26th July 1944 age 32 son of Ernest and Edith Tyrell, Husband of Ivy Tyrell of Sunbury.
Mouen Churchyard
WALKER Bdr. Walter 4039914 21st July 1944 son of Albert and Florence Walker of Holly Hall, Dudley, Husband of Emmie Walker.

BELGIUM
Brussels Town Cemetery
ADAMS Gunner Alfred 4040317 18th Sept 1944 age 24 son of William and Gladys, Husband of Dulcie of Leverton Lincs.
COLES Gunner Francis John 1112477 14th Sept.1944 age 36 son of John and Alice Coles, Husband of Doris Coles of Slough Bucks.
Gheel War Cemetery
ADAMS Gunner Edgar John Cecil 1152705 17th Sept 1944 age 40 son of William and Jane, Husband of Doris of Maidenhead Berks.
EVANS Gunner Thomas James 4040133 17th Sept 1944 age 35 son of William and Clara, Husband of Mary of Froome Herefordshire.
Kasterlee War Cemetery
ARMSTRONG Gunner John 4039899 16th Sept 1944 age 32 son of Thomas and Mary of Cotteridge Warks.

HOLLAND
Jonkerbos War Cemetery
MARLOW Gunner Edmund Ted. 14358480 10th Feb 1945 age 30 son of Edmund and Martha Marlow, Husband of Irene of Clarenden Park Leics.
Neederweert War Cemetery
GIBBONS Gunner Alfred Edward 1152731 2nd Nov.1944 age 45 son of Henry and Elizabeth, Husband of Isabella of Brixton London.
MARKLEW L/Bdr. Cyril 4040577 17th Nov. 1944 age 34 son of Walter and Sarah Husband of Florence of Tetenhall.
Venray War Cemetery
MILLS Gunner Frederick 4040581 5th Dec 1944 age 36 son of Frederick and Anne, Husband of Lucy of Hanley, Stoke on Trent.
NEVILLE Gunner Thomas Edward 4040291 5th Dec 1944 age 24 son of Harold and Violet, of Newport Salop.

GERMANY
Hanover War Cemetery
EVANS Bdr. Edward 1109358 12th April 1945 age 35 son of William and Catherine, Husband of Vera of Rhuddlan,Flintshire.
Reichswald Forest War Cemetery
EVANS Gunner William Howard 4134570 25th March 1945 age 26
Hamburg War Cemetery
FORREST Gunner James 4040139 9th May 1945 age 30.
SHARP Major Stamford Murray 62478 22nd Oct. 1945 age 33 son of James and Clara Husband of Dorothy of Bramhall Cheshire.

Appendix 5

CIRCUMSTANCES OF DEATH

The following notes, cover, briefly the circumstances in which these fatalities were sustained. Accounts have been taken from the War Diaries, and from the men who were there.

3rd August 1940: CONDLIFFE pte. John 4040395, WATERHOUSE pte. Ephraim 4040713. These two men were killed in a road traffic accident. Being the first casualties to the Battalion, their deaths were recalled by several of the men I interviewed.

10th November 1940: BRIDGEWATER Pte. WM. 4040332 Entry from War Diary reads Pte Bridgewater Z Coy. Died while marching back from Armistice day parade. No further explanation.

11th November 1940: VENN L/Cpl. Henry 4040690 Entry from War diary reads : "L/Cpl. Venn Killed whilst acting as DR. (Despatch Rider) after skidding on ice." Two casualties on consecutive days.

9th March 1941: MEREDITH 2/Lt. CC. 126982 Entry from War Diary (timed at 1315) reads: "2/Lt. CC. Meredith found dead in billet in locked room. Cause of death - revolver shot. Arrangements made for inquest at 1530 hrs 10th March 1941. Next of Kin (wife) notified by telegram." All of the Officers who were in the Battalion at the time remember this very tragic incident.

11th November 1942: PRICE Gnr MD. 40400041 Entry from War Diary reads: Gnr. MD. Price Died in Hospital of Sub - Testinal obstruction, officially the first fatal casualty to the 181st Field Regiment. His number is only 13 removed from my Dads, which indicates he would probably have enlisted into the 6th KSLI 17th July 1940.

18th May 1943: WILLIS Gnr. S. 4922849 PACE Gnr. FR. 11562
I discovered a paper in Regimental Orders, covering an enquiry into a serious truck accident, both men killed. Also fatally injured :

19th May 1943: TEDSTONE Gnr.SJ. 4927108. Who died from his injuries the following day.

12th November 1943: LYALL Lt. DB. Entry from War Diary reads: "Lt. DB. Lyall was killed in an accident to vehicle undergoing waterproofing trials."

25th June 1944: GUNN Sgt. AE. 750081: McMORLAND Gnr. R. 1790965: WHEATON Gnr. S. 11002878. Were all killed together, during Gun Drill the day before Operation 'Epsom' began. when a German Artillery shell landed in the gun pit. Three others plus one Officer were seriously wounded. This incident is fully covered in my account.

26th June 1944: CORY-WRIGHT Capt. AJJ. 72690 The first day in Battle, and the Regiment lost its only Officer, killed in action. Julian Cory-Wright joined the Regiment, only 5 days after the conversion, from HQ. RA. 54 Div. and was Adjutant up to the invasion, when he took command of B Troop 177 Bty. ironically, He was moving up on foot, so as not to raise any dust and bring attention to himself, to recce his FOP. position, It was in vain, as his party was hit by either a mortar bomb or shell. It was reported by the NCO., Signal Sgt. Bramald that the Captain's only concern was for his men.

1st July 1944: CORDELL Bdr. VR. 4039928 Was Signaller with Cory - Wright's party, and died of wounds. He was one of the June 1940, intake of men into the 6th Bn. KSLI.

17th July 1944: POUTNEY L/Bdr. RH. 4040601 In modern parlance, would be described as having been killed by 'friendly fire'. A Gunner with 178 Bty. was killed when a shell from a rearward Battery exploded in amongst tree tops surrounding D Troop and 'Dick' was hit by shrapnel in the back and shoulders.

26th July 1944: TYRELL Gnr. JA. 1148922 One of the Regiment's Artillery intake. He was killed when his own sten gun was discharged accidentally. Reputed to have cost 7/6d (37p) to make during the war. The original models were without a safety catch, and prone to go off at the slightest bump, as many old soldiers will testify.

17th/18th September 1944: ADAMS Gnr. A. 4040317, EVANS Gnr. TJ. 4040133
ADAMS Gnr. EJ. 115207. Two Ex-KSLI and an Artilleryman, all Signallers. Killed while attempting to take radio parts up to an FOP. A real Tragedy for 'Charlie' Troop and the Regiment. Gnr. Bill Smith told me that a few hours later the Germans pulled back. The account is recorded in Sgt. Fletcher's Diary, who, with a party, which included my Dad, recovered the bodies under cover of darkness.

17th November 1944: MARKLEW L/Bdr. C. 4040577
He was the Regiment's Medical Orderly who was killed in a minefield. The circumstances of him being there are unclear, but it seems he went out to rescue one of his comrades.

18th November 1944: LOWDON Capt. CSR. (RAMC) 252488 Not strictly on the Roll of the 181st Field Regiment, but was attached and must be included. He was a popular and respected MO. (Medical Officer) Known to all the men. Only 24 years old he was posted to the Regiment on St. Georges day, 23rd April 1943. Along with a party of Officers and men Capt. Lowdon had gone out to recover the body of his Orderly,(L/Bdr. Marklew see above), when he too stepped on a mine.

5th December 1944: MILLS Gnr. F. 4040581 Frederick Mills known to his comrades as 'Paddy'. Was prior to the War a professional footballer for Leeds Utd, and a strong member of the Regimental Football Team. The story goes that Paddy had found most of a German Machine Gun, and was keen to complete his trophy. The Regiment was in convoy and had come to a halt in a 'taped' route through a minefield. Suddenly, Paddy was heard to shout, *"thats just what I'm looking for"* or words to that effect. He jumped out of the lorry, and into the minefield. It's not clear whether he stepped on a mine, or the box he picked up was booby trapped, but Paddy was killed instantly. Percy Lewis, Fred Parsons, and my Dad were in the same lorry.

25th March 1945: EVANS Gnr. WH. 4134570 From D Troop 178 Bty. Killed in action when his Bren Carrier took a direct hit from a German 88mm Gun. Whilst at an FOP.

12th April 1945: EVANS Bdr. E. 1109358 Another, killed by his own Sten Gun, as he went to retrieve a German truck. An eye-witness reported that the bullet entered his thigh and travelled up and into his stomach. Despite surgery he died from his wound. Made all the more tragic as the war had been over for some time.

9th May 1945: FORREST Gnr. J. 4040139 He must be one of the most unfortunate fatalities. Once in Germany the men were billeted in Civilian houses, there wasn't much beer to go round and straws were drawn for one of the few kegs. Jim's house won the beer. Percy Lewis told me, the men stayed up most of the night drinking and playing cards. Poor Jim was found dead the next morning, having choked on his own vomit.

2nd October 1945: SHARPE Maj. SM. 62478 The War Diary entry reads: "Major Sharpe died in hospital from Infantile Paralysis." I have some letters written by Capt Meredith, covering the period during Major Sharpe's illness, describing everyone's sadness and shock that having survived so much he should die in hospital, and only a couple of weeks before he was due to leave the Army.

Appendix 6

HONOURS AND AWARDS

This list of Officers and men has been compiled from the Field Return of Officers the original Documents of Recommendations at the Public Records Office and Ex-personnel's notes. It is important to point out that none of these sources was complete, and while every effort has been made, it is possible that there may be some omissions.

36294	T/Lt/Col	BETHELL	Brian Wyndham		D.S.O.
164853	WS/Lt(T/Capt)	SHAW	Alfred Dudley George		D.S.O.
58015	T/Maj	BROWNE	Archibald Rivers Swinton		M.C.
137103	WSCapt (T/Maj)	CUNIS	JS		M.C.
49828	WS/Capt (T/Maj)	GRAHAME	Geoffrey Charles		M.C.
44862	WS/Capt (T/Maj)	GORLE	Richard Ambrose		M.C.
156684	WS/Lt (T/Capt)	PRUTTON	Nigel Winter		M.C.
156684	WS/Lt (A/Capt)	WARD	Roger Bernard		M.C.
177831	T/Capt	MEREDITH	John		M.C.
4040262	WS/Bdr.	ASPLEY	George Samuel		M.M.
1154332	WS/Bdr.	BROOK	Wallace		M.M.
4040161	WS/Bdr.	JENNINGS	Kenneth Maurice		M.M.
1130277	PA/Bdr.	DYTHAM	Robert Albert		M.M.
1129193	Gnr.	JONES	Melvyn		M.M.
70743	Major	ATTEWELL	P.	LG. 10/05/45	M.I.D.
58015	T/Maj.	BROWNE	ARS	LG. 22/03/45	M.I.D.
4040366	Gnr.	BROOMHALL	P.	LG. 10/05/45	M.I.D.
49828	WS/Capt (T/Maj)	GRAHAME	GC.	LG. 11/10/45	M.I.D.
38398	Lt.Col.	KEENE	TP.	LG. 03/11/45	M.I.D.
177831	T/Capt.	MEREDITH	John	LG. 22/03/45	M.I.D.
244788	Capt.	SHAW	JT.	LG. 04/04/45	M.I.D.
268766	Lieut.	WHIPP	FE.	LG. 10/05/45	M.I.D.
4040366	Gnr.	BROOMHALL	Percy		M.I.D.
	Bdr.	BRANNAN	Cyril		CinC's cert
	Gnr.	JACKSON			CinC's cert
6355288	L/Bdr.	SMITH	Albert		CinC's cert*

Commander in Chiefs Certificate

164853	WS/Lt(T/Capt)	SHAW	ADG	Croix de Guerre
Citation	03/04/45	Avec etoile de vermeil		

Appendix 7

RECOMMENDATIONS FOR AWARDS

36294 BETHELL Richard Brian Wyndham T/Lt.Col. 181 Field Regt. RA.
44th Bde. 15th(S) Div. Recc. 23rd Sept. 1944: DSO (Immediate) LG. 1st Mar. 1945

On the 14th Sept '44 the 44(L) Inf.Bde. affected a ferry crossing of the JUNCTION CANAL, 180ft wide, north of GHEEL and formed a small bridgehead. Lt.Col. BETHELL's Regt. was in close support and he was deputed RA representative for the fire of the Divisional artillery for this operation.

He quickly realised that any increase of enemy pressure would produce a critical situation, unless the Artillery observation and defensive fire plan were rapidly perfected. The ferry was subjected to continuous small arms fire and considerable shell fire, and throughout the afternoon and night many small boats were sunk and casualties sustained. Lt.Col. BETHELL then crossed and re-crossed this canal into the bridgehead, which at this time was about a mile square. Here he organised his arty. observation posts and prepared defensive plans while still under fire, giving confidence and guidance to his juniors in close touch with the enemy.

That night the enemy counter attacked. They were repulsed by the defensive artillery fire bought down by Lt.Col. BETHELL. The bridgehead was then reduced to an area of less than 400 yards square. No bridge was yet built and the situation was critical. Casualties had been sustained and the Artillery observation posts had been considerably disorganised and equipment damaged by enemy fire. Lt.Col. BETHELL again organised personally the observation and fire plan, under increased and heavy enemy fire. The following night the enemy again attacked in strength the bridgehead garrison, whose only link to the rear was by three boats. The effective and immediate artillery fire bought down as a direct result of Lt.Col. BETHELL's continuous and tireless efforts averted a heavy attack on tired Troops. Many casualties were inflicted on the enemy who withdrew after repeated attempts. For two days after this he continued to protect the bridgehead in this manner. His coolness, and the skill of him and those under him may well have averted a serious reverse. His good services were of the highest order, and his devotion to duty worthy of the highest traditions of the service.

164853 SHAW Alfred George Dudley WS/Lt. (T/Capt) 181 Field Regt RA.
44th(L) Bde. 15th(S) Div. Recc. 3rd March 1945: DSO (Immediate) LG. 8th May 1945

Between the 8th and 26th Feb '45 Capt. SHAW was OP. Offr. supporting 6 KOSB. in the attack on GROESBEEK Eastwards through the SEIGFRIED LINE. On 9th Feb 6 KOSB were ordered to cross the main a/tk obstacle at KRANNENBURG. Capt SHAW acted as CO's rep. and on him devolved the planning of the arty. support. Moving with the fwd. elements of the inf. approaching the objective heavy shell and mortar fire made progress impossible.

Capt. SHAW coolly evolved the immediate arty. plan and by it enabled the inf. to continue the adv. and capture the objective. Later, Capt. SHAW was moving with the leading coy. 6 KOSB in their attack on the high ground SE. of GOCH. On the way to his first objective his carrier became bogged and was heavily shelled. Capt. SHAW dismounted and, collecting a tank had his carrier towed to the objective. There he found the coy. comd. had become separated from his coy. The 2i/c killed and the inf. wireless set knocked out. Having established his OP. Ieaving his OPA. in it, he set about re-organising the coy. He took also his 18 set and put it on the Bn. net. From then for about an hour he commanded the coy. sent back vital news as to the progress of the battle to the Bn. cmd. and at the same time engaged by observation, targets on the right flank which were holding up the advance to the second objective. Again moving forward with the coy. he est. an OP. which commanded a view of the main enemy axis on the HOST-WEEZE Rd. Though light was failing he bought heavy and concentrated fire on enemy vehicles congested in ROTTUM causing considerable destruction and many casualties. Capt. SHAW remained in this OP for 40 hours giving continuous and vital information on enemy movement though subjected himself to severe enemy shelling and spasmodic inf. attacks. Throughout the whole operation, though without sleep or rest for long periods, Capt SHAW'S courage. initiative and acceptance of responsibility much above his normal duty, and his skill in handling a large number of guns enabled the inf. to continue their advance. The endurance and devotion to duty of this officer under adverse conditions were beyond all praise.

58015 BROWNE Archibald Rivers Swinton T/Maj. 181 Field Regt RA.
44th(L)Bde. 15th(S) Div. Recc. 23rd Sept. 1944 MC (Imm): LG. 1st Mar. 1945

On the 14th Sept. 1944 the 8th Royal Scots formed a bridgehead across the JUNCTION CANAL at GHEEL this produced increasingly heavy enemy reaction in this area and the problem of arty. observation and support became increasingly difficult. The vital link in bringing the weight of the Div. arty. on this all but beleaguered area lay in Major BROWNE commanding a field arty. bty. in support of the Royal Scots. For reasons of communications and to give physical and moral help to his OP's. he established his position at the bridgehead crossing. This area was continually and increasingly under fire. For three days Major BROWNE worked unceasingly to give the arty. support necessary. He made repeated crossings of the canal under fire to visit his OP's on one occasion his boat being sunk by enemy fire. He affected the co-ordination of the highest standard of arty. work in the bridgehead which enabled many counter attacks to be repulsed which caused many enemy casualties. Throughout Major BROWNE was continually in the bridgehead area deporting himself with a complete disregard for enemy shellfire. His imperturbable bearing and cheerful humour under fire encouraging all who saw him. His fine example of courage and endurance was of the most distinguished character.

137103 CUNIS Jack Sydney WS/Capt. 181 Field Regt RA.
44th(L) Inf.Bde. 15th(S) Div. Recc. 25th June 1945 MC (Periodic): LG. 24th Jan. 1946

This Officer has been with the Regt throughout the campaign in NW Europe and has taken part in every major operation usually as an OP Officer with the leading infantry. His ability to bring down fire with maximum effect in the minimum of time, while himself exposed to enemy fire of all sorts, not only once, but always when he was in a position to do so, has most certainly had a tremendous effect on the successful outcome of each operation. In the GOCH area Capt. CUNIS although he had a good OP from which he could carry out his immediate job found another which though extremely exposed and dangerous enabled him also to fire on enemy transport further back. While in this OP. he was approached by two enemy SP. guns which fired at his OP and nearby infantry. He directed accurate and observed fire on these which was so successful that they were forced to withdraw. This is a typical instance of Capt. CUNIS's bravery and initiative which has been an inspiration to those working under him and earned the absolute confidence of the infantry whom he has supported so gallantly.

44862 GORLE Richard Ambrose WS/Capt T/Maj. 181 Field Regt. RA.
44th(L) Bde. 15th (S) Div. Recc. 9th Dec. 1944 MC (1mm): LG. 5th Apr. 1944

On 3rd. Dec. Maj. GORLE was the arty. rep. with the 6th Bn. RSF. in the attack on BLERICK by 15(S)Div. The objective lay beyond a wide stretch of open ground crossed by enemy dug - in defences and an A/Tk. ditch. This in turn was overlooked by the enemy located in the outskirts of BLERICK. His position was one of Great responsibility, involving the direction of many guns and the subduing of unlocated enemy positions. Moving to the attack with the leading infantry Maj. GORLE soon realised that the necessary recce. for vital OP's could not be carried out in his vehicle in such open country. Maj. GORLE repeatedly left his 'kangaroo' in which vehicles the attacking Troops were mounted, and well knowing the area to be mined, he walked under heavy fire to find suitable viewpoints and to keep in close touch with the operation, this he continued to do throughout the day. By his disregard for his own safety, and by his resource, he was able to continue to play his vital part in the battle until the objective was gained.

49828 GRAHAME Geoffrey Charles WS/Capt. T/Maj; 181 field Regt RA.
44th(L) Inf. Bde. 15th(S) Div. Recc. 10th May 1945 MC (Periodical): LG. 11th Nov. 1945

Throughout the period 1st Feb to 30th Apr. Major GRAHAME has commanded 178 Fd.Bty. and has taken part in the following actions: Breaching of the SEIGFRIED LINE and advance to CLEVE and GOCH: Crossing of the RHINE and advance to ISSEL:

UELZEN and the crossing of the River ELBE. In every one of these Major GRAHAME by his resource and coolness under fire has ensured maximum support for 6th Bn. KOSB. whom his bty. supports. In the advance of the 44th Inf.Bde. from the RHINE to the ISSEL his behaviour was particularly outstanding. Though his driver was killed when his carrier was hit by shellfire he nevertheless got forward under steady shell and mortar fire and ensured that adequate arty. fire was bought down to hold off a strong enemy counter attack. His determination was very largely responsible for the fact that the enemy attack was beaten back with considerable loss by artillery fire. He has throughout set a very fine example to all ranks and displayed quite outstanding leadership.

177831 MEREDITH John Temp/Capt. 181 Field Regt RA.
44th(L) Bde. 15th(S) Recc. 23rd Sept. 1944 MC (Imm): LG. 1st Mar. 1945

On the 14th and 15th Sept 1944 Capt. MEREDITH was acting arty. observer in the GHEEL Bridgehead. The area was so restricted that it offered to him one suitable OP. in a church spire. Repeated enemy counter attacks were repulsed as a result of his observation and the value of his work was soon recognised by the enemy who bought his OP. under continuous shellfire. In spite of this Capt. MEREDITH remained to carry out his work. In due course he was wounded in the leg, and his wireless set was destroyed by a direct hit. He went to the Bn. HQ of the KOSB and obtained another wireless set and continued under heavy fire to continue his work from one of the few houses left standing near the church. Here he remained and not until nightfall did he give thought to his wound or ask for relief. By daylight Capt. MEREDITH had again occupied his OP. Which in turn had been bought under fire heavy enemy fire. Whilst observing fire on another enemy counter attack this OP. too was destroyed by enemy shellfire. Though suffering from shock Capt. MEREDITH again established communications and continued to order defensive fire as required by the situation. On the relief of the Bn. he recrossed the canal in the last boat. His splendid example of endurance, courage and devotion to duty was an inspiration to all and was a vital contribution to the holding of the GHEEL bridgehead.

1S6684 PRUTTON Nigel Winter WS/LT. T/Capt. 181 Field Regt. RA.
44th(L) Inf.Bde. 15th(S) Div. Recc. 21st Oct. 1944 MC (Imm): LG. 1st Mar. 1945

On Sept 27th 6 RSF attacked to secure an objective in the area NW of ODENRODE. Capt. PRUTTON accompanied by the leading company as FOO. Considerable difficulty in reaching the objective resulted in all the Officers in company Headquarters becoming casualties. On his own initiative he assumed command of the company and took control of the situation. At this time all communications of the forward companies were out of action. Capt. PRUTTON continued throughout the whole operation and until the objective was reached to send back valuable information as to the situation of the forward companies to the battalion commander. All this he did in addition to his orders to his artillery for defensive fire which was responsible for the infantry reaching their objective. His initiative and conduct under heavy fire and his complete disregard for his own safety bought confidence in all those around him and his example was an inspiration to the infantry.

220938 WARD Roger Bernard WS/Lt A/Capt. 181 Field Regt. RA.
44th(L) Inf.Bde. 15th(S) Div. Recc. 9th Dec. 1944 MC (Imm): LG. 5th Apr. 1945

On the 3rd dec. Capt. WARD was the arty. FOO. in the attack by the 15th (s)Div. on BLERICK. The objective lay beyond a wide stretch of open ground crossed by enemy dug-in defences and an A/TK ditch. This was in turn overlooked by the enemy located in the outskirts of BLERICK. Moving in his tank at the head of the attacking echelon he established himself on the A/TK. obstacle where concealment was impossible. Here he stayed throughout the day under heavy field and medium enemy fire and displayed a splendid example of endurance, directing throughout the fire of our arty. with the utmost skill and initiative. His continued efforts on the more vital flank of the attack materially contributed to the success of the operation and earned the highest praise from the infantry whom he was supporting. During the action Capt. WARD's position was rendered precarious by enemy fire from a nearby house. This he engaged with his 6-pounder gun, silencing the enemy. Dismounting and on foot he proceeded along the A/TK. ditch. Here he captured 5 of the enemy and then the occupants of the house.

4040262 ASPLEY George Samuel WS/Bdr. 181 Field Regt. RA.
44th(L) Inf.Bde. 15th(S) Div. 12 Corps Recc. 23rd Sep. 1944 MM (Imm): LG. 1st Mar. 1945

15th -16th Sept '44 JUNCTION CANAL 0793. For two days Bdr. Aspley was a Signaller in an OP. in the canal bridgehead. The whole position was under continual shellfire. First one OP. then another was knocked out, all the wireless sets were destroyed. Two teams of OP. Signallers were hit by shellfire, Bdr ASPLEY was slightly wounded and shaken by blast. In spite of this however he acted as runner between his OP. Officer and Bn. HQ. where the only wireless set in communication with the guns was situated, and by repeated journeys he enabled effective arty.fire to be bought down. The street down which he had to pass was under continual shellfire and partial observation by the enemy. Throughout the whole action Bdr. Aspley's conduct was a fine example of outstanding courage and devotion to duty and his action contributed in no small manner to the holding of the bridgehead.

1154332 BROOK Wallace WS/Bdr. 181 Field Regt RA.
44th(L) Bde. 15th(S) Div. 12 corps Recc. 11th May 1945 MM (Periodic): LG. 11th Oct. 1945

WS/Bdr. BROOK has been NCO. i/c Bty.comd. sig. party over a long period both before and including 1st Feb - 31st March 1945. Through all this period the vital communications of the B/C with his OP's and with his Regtl. HQ. have never failed despite continuous long stretches when both wireless and line communications have been under heavy shell and mortar fire and both have, on several occasions been hit and temporarily put out of action. It has been through the cool determination and devotion to duty of this NCO. that at no time has the B/C been without communications. In the IJSELL bridgehead when the Bty.was supporting 6 RSF. the Battery in the OP. was hit and destroyed Bdr. BROOK well knowing the route to the OP. to be exposed to continuous shellfire and small arms fire and in view of the enemy volunteered to take up a fresh Battery. Despite the shellfire Bdr. BROOK reached a point very close to the OP. before being himself wounded thus enabling the Signaller at the OP. to move back a short distance and re-established wireless communication. By his excellent example and leadership this NCO. has maintained a high standard of efficiency and excellent morale amongst his signal team throughout the whole campaign.

1130277 DYTHAM Robert Albert P/A/Bdr. 181 Field Regt. RA.
44th(L) Bde. 15th(S) Div. Recc. 23rd Sept. 1944 MM (Imm): LG. 1st March 1945

On the 15th Sept. 1944 inf.Bde. made an assault crossing of the JUNCTION CANAL at GHEEL. Bdr. DYTHAM was in charge of the communications of an OP. team supporting the assault. Although the heavy shelling and mortaring of the area between the OP. and carrier was one of great danger, Bdr. DYTHAM first carried his remote control across this area a distance of 200 yds to a point where his arty.fire could be observed. Having done this he returned to the carrier to fetch an accumulator which he again carried to the OP. This was blown out of his hands by enemy fire, and though shaken by its effect, he again returned for a second accumulator. Again under fire he returned to the OP. and succeeded this time in establishing the communications which were vital to the success of the assault. During the battle, he continued his journeys under frequent and heavy shelling ensuring that good communications were maintained by his complete disregard for his own safety, and by devotion to duty Bdr. DYTHAM enabled the fire of the arty. to be bought down without delay throughout the operation and his fine work contributed greatly to its success.

4040161 JENNINGS Kenneth Maurice WS/Bdr. 181 Field Regt. RA.
44th(L) Bde. 15th(S) Div. 12 Corps Recc. 23rd Sept. 1944 MM (Imm): LG. 1st Mar. 1945

On 14th Sept. Bdr. JENNINGS was in charge of communications and men of an arty. OP team which accompanied the assault Troops crossing the JUNCTION CANAL at GHEEL his duties as such and the nature of the operation rendered his work and intention vital to its success. Bdr. JENNINGS organised his party and took it into action by boat and having established communications he maintained them steadily under fire continuously and efficiently for 48 hrs. This involved frequent journeys between the WT. set and the OP. in an area at times when enemy fire had forced all other Troops under cover. The frequent moves of the OP. due to shellfire made his work more hazardous and difficult. A hit on the WT. set necessitated its replacement and Bdr. JENNINGS led a party back across the canal and carried forward a new set with which he regained communication with his Bty. As a direct result of Bdr. JENNINGS sustained efforts under fire, successful arty. fire was bought to bear on the enemy. His leadership and example were responsible for the splendid and willing work of his team. The effect which the bearing and conduct of Bdr. JENNINGS had on all Gunners around him while under fire cannot be overstated. He materially influenced the operation.

1129193 JONES Melvyn Gunner 181 Field Regt. RA.
44th(L) Inf.Bde. 15th(S) Inf. Div. Recc. 10th May 1945 MM (Periodic): LG. 11th Oct. 1945

From 1st Feb - 30th April 1945 Gnr. MELVYN JONES has been Signaller to the Bty. Comd. 178 Bty. During this period the Bty has supported 6 Bn. KOSB. in all the actions including the SIEGFRIED LINE, CLEVE and GOCH, the RHINE crossing and advance to IJSSELL, UELZEN, and the crossing of the ELBE. As B/C's Signaller, JONES was responsible for communications on which all fire support for the Bn. depended and he has consistently kept them open often in the most hazardous conditions, notably in the area of GOCH was his behaviour outstanding the aerial of one set was shot away and later the vehicle itself was hit and the set destroyed by enemy shellfire. JONES each time effected the necessary repairs and replacements though it meant working in an exposed position under heavy fire. The fine example of this very young soldier has had an incalculable effect in keeping everyone with whom he came into contact imbued with the same spirit as his own.

Lt. Bill Busby - then

Bill Busby - now

Gnr/Sig. Bill Smith - then
Showing the details of divisional sign
And regimental 'gold bugle' badge.

Bill Smith - now

Gnr/Dvr. Charlie Ashton - then   Charlie Ashton - recently (since deceased)

Gnr/Dvr. Charlie Spence - then   Charlie Spence - now

Lt. Wladyslaw Rolski and David Small - then

David Small - now

L/Cpl. Fred Parsons - then

Fred Parsons - now

Bdr. George Aspley MM - then

George Aspley - recently (since deceased)

Gnr. John May - then

John May - now

Major Shaw - then. Receiving his DSO with his wife Dorothy at Buckingham Palace.

J Telfer DCM and ADG Shaw DSO - now Taken at 44 Bde reunion - France

Lt. Philip Mulholland - then

Philip Mulholland - now

Maj John Meredith MC - then   John Meredith - recently (since deceased)

Gnr/Dvr Percy Lewis - then   Percy Lewis - recently (since deceased)

Capt. Tommy Stokes - then

Tommy Stokes - now

L/Sgt. Ted Eden - then

Ted Eden - now

Waiting to cross the Elbe. OP Team 177 Bty, L/R Gnrs Ballymont, Coe, Temple, Bdr Goy.

Drivers C Troop Holland 1944. L/R Gnr Lewis, Sgt Gibbons, Gnr Basnett, Gnr Cotton.

C/Sub gun crew, near Ueltzen, L/R Gnr Rowlands,
Bdr Fornknall, Gnr Kilby, Gnr Hardy, Sig Abbis

River Elbe March 1945. A group of NCO's, L/R, Sgt Onions, Bdr Jennings,
BSM Saunders, Sgt Edwards. Jennings was awarded the MM for exceptional service.

L. Gnr/Dvr 'Sonny' Cotton, R. Gnr/Dvr. McInerie. McInerie joined with a contingent of men including Charlie Spence from 6th Field Training Regt. A good photo showing how the 'Tam' should and shouldn't be worn! Also note the detail of the Soldiers webbing.

Sgt. Edmund Linard and Sgt. 'Dick' Fletcher. Both ex-regular KSLI Soldiers. At his own request Sgt. Linard was transferred to the Infantry (6 RSF). Tragically, only weeks later he was killed by his own guns during the Rhine crossing, when a 'short shell' knocked out half of his platoon. A fine photograph. All the Officers I speak to pay fine tribute to the Regiment's NCO's.

15th Scottish Crest

Presented to

Sergeant Richard FLETCHER

by

COMMANDER 15ᵀᴴ SCOTTISH DIVISION

in recognition of Gallant Service and devotion
to duty during the Campaign from NORMANDY
to the ELBE in 1944/45

MAJOR GENERAL
COMMANDING 15ᵀᴴ SCOTTISH DIVISION

Commander-in-Chiefs Certificate, awarded to Sgt Dick Fletcher.

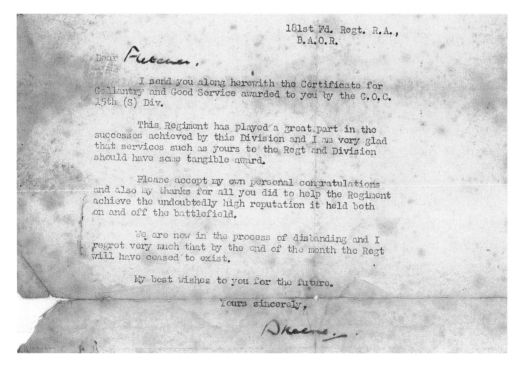

181st Fd. Regt. R.A.,
B.A.O.R.

Dear Fletcher,

I send you along herewith the Certificate for
Gallantry and Good Service awarded to you by the G.O.C.
15th (S) Div.

This Regiment has played a great part in the
successes achieved by this Division and I am very glad
that services such as yours to the Regt and Division
should have some tangible award.

Please accept my own personal congratulations
and also my thanks for all you did to help the Regiment
achieve the undoubtedly high reputation it held both
on and off the battlefield.

We are now in the process of disbanding and I
regret very much that by the end of the month the Regt
will have ceased to exist.

My best wishes to you for the future.

Yours sincerely,

Accompanying letter from C/O 181 Field Regiment RA.

Military Medal - Awarded to George Aspley.

My father's insignia and medals, including National Service
and Normandy Veterans commemorative medals.

Medals, Badges and Insignia worn by the men of 6 KSLI - 181 Field Regt. RA.

Badges and Insignia of the units that fought with the 15th Scottish Division.

Campagnes pour la libération de la France

(Juin - Décembre 1944)

Décision N° 589

Le Général de Gaulle,
Président du Gouvernement Provisoire de la
République Française,

Cite à l'Ordre DU CORPS d'ARMEE :

WS/Lt (T/Capt) Alfred Dudley George SHAW 164853 RA

181 Fd Regt RA - 44 Bde 15 Div

" *Pour services exceptionnels de Guerre rendus au*
" *cours des opérations de libération de la France.*"

Cette Citation comporte l'attribution de la Croix de
Guerre avec Etoile de Vermeil

PARIS, le 3 Avril 1945

Citation for the Croix de Guerre awarded to Capt ADG Shaw.

Appendix 8

DISPOSITION OF OFFICERS

6th Bn. K.S.L.I. 7/4/1941

Bn. headquarters

C.O. Lt/Col.	RBS Munn
Lt.	JS. Woods
Lt.	EW. Corbett
Lt.	WM. Busby
Lt.Q.M.	GW. Norton
2/Lt.	RN. Cooke

H.Q. Company

PRI.	Maj.	LS. Munn
Adjt.	2/Lt.	DN. McOwan
	(SO)	No.1 Pl. Comm.
I/O.	2/Lt.	KA. Gardener
Mortar	Off.	No.3 Pl. Comm.
W.T.O.	2/Lt.	JR. Jacques
Carrier	Off.	No.4 Pl. Comm.
Mess.Off.2/Lt.		EV Matthewman
		No. 4 Pl.
M.T.O. Capt.		RG. Maurice
		No. 6 Pl.

W Company

Capt.	JL. Martin
Capt. 2.i/c.	JA. Grischotti
2/Lt	PB. Warneford
2/Lt.	DL. Blois
2/Lt.	GA. Thompson
2/Lt.	KA. Hyne

X Company

Cy.Com.	Capt.	RG. Bristowe
2i/c.	2/Lt.	WN. Moore
	2/Lt.	NW. Prutton
	2/Lt.	ADG. Shaw
	2/Lt.	JT. Gibbons
	2/Lt.	HM. Godfrey

Y Company

Capt.	JA. Aitken Coy.Comm.
2/Lt. 2i/c.	JS. Shields
2/Lt.	TED. Paddock
2/Lt.	J. Meredith
2/Lt.	JC. Wright

Z Company

	Maj.	LG.Day Coy. Comm.
2i/c.	Capt.	FR. Whitwell
	2/Lt.	BF. Murtagh
	2/Lt.	PW. Haydon
	2/Lt.	P. Young

Appendix 9

204TH INDEPENDENT INFANTRY BRIGADE (HOME)

October 1940 :   Formed for service in the U.K. by No.4 Infantry Training Group
25th Nov.1941:   Redesignated 204th Independent Infantry Brigade

1st Sept. 1942:   Brigade H.Q. redesignated H.Q.185th Infantry Brigade

Commanding Officers

12th Oct. 1940: Brigadier General M. Bruce
21 Aug. 1942: Lt.col. PDS. Palmer (acting)

Units Under Command

7th Bn. South Lancashire Regt.	12.10.40 - 31.8.42
8th Bn. South Lancashire Regt	12.10.40 - 31.5.41
12th Bn.Sherwood Foresters	12.10.40 - 31.8.42
6th Bn. King's Shropshire Light Inf.	**12.10.40 - 24.11.41**
7th Bn. Leicestershire Regt.	26.11.41 - 31.8.42

Higher Formations Served Under

North Midlands	12.10.40 - 26.3.41
Lincoln county division	27.3.41 - 24.11.41
Durham & North Riding Coastal Area	25.11.41 - 31.8.42

Theatre

United Kingdom   12.10.40 - 31.8.42

Appendix 10

THE FINAL ROLL OF OFFICERS 6TH BN. KSLI

Those who elected to remain with the Infantry, and those who elected to transfer to the newly formed 181st Field Regt RA

Taken from R.O. 3/3/42

The following Officers were attached to 181 Field Regiment on the 1/3/42 pending re - posting to Infantry units :

56717	A/Maj.	AM.Askwith	p61048	L/Col.	RBS. Munn
126979	Lt.	EC. Curtis	p34669	T/Maj.	D.Colville
162622	2/Lt.	PW. Haydon	p157920	T/Capt.	JS. Woods
126983	T/Capt.	WN. Moore	176349	2/Lt.	EV. Matthewman
201826	2/Lt.	J. Neilson	137676	Lt.	GW. Norton
117833	2/Lt.	JC. Wright	207827	2/Lt.	J. Wilson
112988	Lt.	JA. Grischotti	112839	Lt.	PJW. Cuckney
126978	Lt.	Rl. Cooke	12190	T/Maj.	LG. Day
49884	Capt.	RJ. Hereford.	203120	2/Lt.	VR. Evans
198245	2/Lt.	PG.Spooner			

The following Officers were attached to 181 Field Regiment on the 1/3/42 pending transfer to the Royal Artillery (subject to suitability) under WO.UM.20/arty/6039/ AGIA.

12236	T/Capt.	RG. Bristowe	1601576	A/Capt.	EW. Corbett
165854	2/Lt.	JT. Gibbons	164674	2/Lt.	JR. Jacques
122263	T/Capt.	JC. Martin	135313	T/Capt.	RG. Maurice
137254	Lt.	DN. McOwen	177831	2/Lt.	J. Meredith
204406	2/Lt	P. Mulholland	156693	2/Lt.	TED. Paddock
156684	2/Lt.	NW. Prutton	203403	2/Lt.	J. Raitz
147239	2/Lt.	JS. Shields	164853	2/Lt.	ADG. Shaw
186293	2/Lt.	LA. Sturley	187117	2/Lt.	TJ. Stokes
187118	2/Lt.	MJ. Walters	161170	2/Lt.	KA. Hyne

Appendix 11

RECORDED POSITIONS OF BHQ

Taken from the War Diary of the 6th Bn. KSLI and the 181st Field Regt RA. Listed below are the recorded positions of BHQ and, in some cases Company Areas.

Date   **Position**

1st October	1940	Wellbeck Abbey
22nd October	1940	Wangley Manor
14th January	1941	Boston
13th February	1941	Skegness
4th March	1941	Spilsby
2nd April	1941	Chapel St. Leonards
29th May	1941	Grimsthorpe
8th June	1941	Tadcaster
11th June	1941	Grimsthorpe Castle
18th June	1941	Chapel St.Leonards
2nd January	1942	Tadcaster / position Louth (On Exercise)
12th January	1942	Coningsby Area :-
		HQ. Tattershall, HQ. Coy. Mareham Le Fen
		W. Coy. Tattershall,
		X. Coy. Old Bollingbrooke
		Y. Coy Woodhall Spa

1st March: Transfer to 181 Field Regiment RA.

3rd March	1942	Melton Mowbray Area :
		RHQ Melton Mowbray / Newport Lodge
		Q Bty. Gaddesby Park Hall
		R Bty. Bagrave Hall
		S Bty. Ashby Folville
July/ August	1942	Ponteland: Newbiggin :Otterburn:
		Friskney for shooting practice.
19th September	1942	Low Lynn
1st November	1942	Berwick on Tweed shooting practice at:
		Longframlington: Emblehope:
		Pockstowe: Hemlinborough:
		Pocklington: Baysdale:
		Osmotherely. RHQ. Nunburnholme.
1st September	1943	Haydon Bridge
3rd November'	1943	Berwick on Tweed
1st January	1944	Harrowgate
16th February	1944	Harrowgate: Bty's returned to
		Nunburnholme and Pocklington, where
		they remained until April, when they
		travelled to Worthington prior to the invasion.

Appendix 12

181 FIELD REGIMENT ROYAL ARTILLERY

1st March 1942 :   Formed largely from the 6th Battalion
                            King's Shropshire Light Infantry
                            Three Batteries: Lettered Q: R: S

11th March 1942   Batteries redesignated: Q: R: P

1st January 1943   Batteries redesignated and numbered:
                            177 :178 :179

9th January 1946   Regiment officially disbanded

Source: Lineage book of British land Regiments

On the 28th February 1942 the 6th Battalion The King's Shropshire Light Infantry ceased to exist, and was converted to the 181st Field Regiment Royal Artillery. After A War Office intelligence test 484 men from the 6th KSLI were transferred into the new Regiment. About 140 men were considered more suitable for the Infantry, and a similar number were transferred to the Pioneer Corps. Those transferred to the the Infantry went to other Battalions KSLI and to the Herefordshire Regiment.

The original Batteries were designated Q: R: S "Q" Bty. would train the Gunners, and particularly gunlayers "R" Bty. would train the drivers "S" Bty. would train the specialists and Signallers

The Batteries would be formed into three Troops each. After a couple of months training one Troop from each Battery would move to another, thus forming three permanent Batteries of mixed skills.

Appendix 13

TRANSFORMATION

On the 28th February 1942 the 6th Battalion King's Shropshire Light Infantry ceased to exist and was converted to the 181st Field Regiment Royal Artillery. 484 other ranks and NCO's were transferred to the newly formed Regiment,

Taken from Daily Orders the complete roll was as follows:

The following were transferred and posted to 181st Regimental Headquarters

4039968	Sgt	Henley	R.	4034497	Sgt.	Palmer	S.	4040007	L/Cpl.	Lewis	E.
4037340	Sgt.	Lilley	A.	4040270	Sgt.	Lloyd	N.	4040734	Sgt.	Furlong	T.
4040577	L/Cpl.	Marklew	C.KIA	4040114	Pte.	Bethell	F.	4040017	Pte.	McIlgrew	F.
4040298	Pte.	Cluett	J.	3523849	Pte.	Meadowcroft	J.	4040388	Pte.	Couta	F.
4039522	Pte.	Chilton	S.	4040257	L/Cpl.	Moyle	T.	4040312	Pte.	Davies	J.
4040041	Pte.	Price	M. KAS	4040263	L/Cpl.	Ebdy	C.	4040639	Cpl.	Roberts	V.
4040258	L/Sgt.	Edwards	G.	4040269	L/Cpl.	Shelley	H.	4040436	Pte.	Evans	W.
4040242	Pte.	Taylor	T.	4040445	Pte.	Floyd	J.	4040241	Pte.	Underwood	H.
4039952	Pte.	Farmer	T.	4040310	Pte.	Wilson	B.	5052521	Pte.	Geeson	R.
4040277	Pte.	Windridge	E.	4031295	Cpl.	Howells	G.	4040249	Pte.	Wakelam	W.
4040239	Pte.	Haddock	A.	4039921	Pte.	Bishop	B.	4040477	Pte.	Heath	N.
4039991	Cpl.	Jeffries	G.	4040334	Pte.	Beardmore	D.	4040413	Pte.	Davies	E.
4040536	Pte.	Judge	E.	4040563	Pte.	Leake	T.	4040528	Pte.	Jones	C.
4040099	Pte.	Ward	C.	4040169	Pte.	Knowles	W.	4040541	Pte.	Kyte	W.

The following were transferred and posted to "Q" Bty 181 Field Regiment RA.

4033942	CQMS	Norcross	J.	4031603	Cpl.	Fletcher	R.	4037362	Sgt.	Owens	O.
4039953	Pte.	Francis	S.	4039894	Pte.	Adam	S.	4039946	Pte.	Garratt	W.
4040348	Pte.	Banks	W.	4040457	Pte.	Gough	W.	4104466	Pte.	Bridges	T.
4040469	Pte.	Gallear	H.	4039928	Cpl.	Cordell	V. KIA	4039972	Pte.	Hallworth	J.
4040377	Pte.	Caddick	S.	4031577	Pte.	Hood	R	4040382	Pte.	Childs	W.
4040481	L/Cpl.	Handley	W.	4040289	L/Cpl.	Clee	G.	4040494	Pte.	Hill	T.
4040415	Pte.	Dunton	H.	4039971	Pte.	Hall	E.	4039939	Pte.	Dugmore	A.
4040476	Pte.	Hodges	G.	4039938	Pte.	Davies	G.	4040502	Pte.	Hill	E.
4040133	Pte.	Evans	T. KIA	4040533	Pte.	Jones	T.	4040431	Pte.	Evans	G.
4040520	Pte.	Jones	S.	4039954	Pte.	Farmer	H.	4039419	Pte.	Jones	T.
4040442	Pte.	Foster	F.	4040001	Pte.	Kinsey	C.	4040136	Pte.	Forknall	H.
4040560	Pte.	Latham	F.	4030731	Cpl.	Grimshaw	J.	4040301	L/Sgt.	Leighton	J.
4040460	Pte.	Goodrich	W.	4040549	Pte.	Lewis	M.	4040455	Pte.	Giles	T.
4040566	Pte.	Lote	J.	4039973	Pte.	Hodgkinson	C.	4040026	Pte.	Maddox	T.
4040266	Pte.	Hill	C.	4040578	L/Cpl.	Mason	C.	4040485	Pte.	Hill	W.
4040178	pte.	Hook	E.	4040148	Pte.	Hazlewood	G.	4030050	Cpl.	Mountford	W.
4039981	Pte.	Hyde	A	4040572	Pte	Morris	W.	4039985	Pte.	Hughes	W.
4040586	Pte.	Myatt	E.	4039987	Cpl.	Ingram	J.	4040593	Pte.	Newmann	J.

4040532	Pte.	Jones	H.	4031581	Cpl.	Powis	M.	4040526	Pte.	Jones	H.
4040630	L/Cpl.	Price	E.	4040159	Pte.	Jones	J.	4040240	Pte.	Parker	F.
4040004	Cpl.	Knight	W.	4040190	Pte.	Plimbley	G.	3653604	Pte.	Lawton	S.
4040620	Pte.	Price	J.	4040014	Pte.	Lewis	P.	4040607	Pte.	Powell	G.
4031935	Cpl.	Linard	E. KIA	4040048	Pte.	Rice	J.	4031471	Pte.	Lane	G.
4040196	Pte.	Robbins	G.	4040251	Pte.	Marston	H.	4040634	Pte.	Rowley	G.
4040233	Pte.	MacMaster	R.	4040054	Pte.	Reed	W.	4040581	Pte.	Mills	F. KIA
4040295	Pte.	Reece	L.	4040022	Pte.	Mullan	A.	4040204	Pte.	Smith	G.
4040180	Pte.	Moulstone	J.	4040058	Pte.	Saunders	G.	4040182	Pte.	Newton	L.
4040063	Pte.	Small	E.	4040028	Pte.	NEAL	G.	4040218	Pte.	Thomas	A.
4040602	Pte.	Peach	H.	4040677	Pte.	Thornton	P.	4040273	Pte.	Poyner	E.
4040684	Pte.	Tunnicliffe	W.	4040046	Pte.	Pardoe	W.	4037406	Cpl.	Tunnicliffe	E.
4040191	Pte.	Peck	J.	4040704	Pte.	Woolrich	W.	4040601	L/Cpl.	Poutney	R. KIA
4032437	L/Sgt.	Watkins	R.	4206788	Pte.	Powell	T.	4040353	Pte.	Butler	W.
4037337	Sgt.	Layton	C.	4040367	Pte.	Bowdler	T.	4040110	Sgt.	Floyd	W.
4040493	Pte.	Chetwood	H.	4040318	Pte.	Aldridge	H.	4040129	Pte.	Evans	H.
4039991	Pte.	Brown	A.	4040139	Pte.	Forrest	J. KAS	4040350	Cpl.	Bennett	I.
4040486	Pte.	Hughes	S.	4040378	Cpl.	Cowern	G.	4040522	Pte.	Jones	A.
4037879	Pte.	Caldicott	W.	4040588	Pte.	Malpass	C.	4037184	Cpl.	Coley	J.
4040261	Cpl.	Chattaway	T.	4030055	Pte.	Parkes	W.	4040412	Pte.	Dawson	H.
4039470	Pte.	Rawlings	S.	4040426	Pte.	Devaney	J.	4206789	Pte.	Reeves	G.
4040429	Pte.	Elliot	S.	4029953	Pte.	Wearing	W.	4030703	Cpl.	Edwards	W.
4040337	Pte.	Burroughs	F.	4040430	Pte.	Ecclestone	H.	4040643	Pte.	Robinson	W.
4040056	Pte.	Rowlands	G.	4040650	Pte.	Summall	J.	4040329	Pte.	Burns	S.
4040659	Pte.	Steele	R.	4039904	Pte.	Barney	E.	4040649	Pte.	Smith	W.
4040375	Pte.	Clee	H.	5124553	Pte.	Slawson	H.	4040450	Pte.	Fowell	A.
4040680	Pte.	Thornley	L.	3961622	Pte.	Gwynne	L.	4040679	Pte.	Tench	S.
4040000	Pte.	Kilminster	T.	4040693	Pte.	Watson	N.	4040023	Pte.	Mills	J.
4039914	Pte.	Walker	W.	4039619	Pte.	O'Grady	G.	4040230	Pte.	Pitchford	G.
4040198	Pte.	Read	J.	4040652	Pte.	Salter	G.	4040228	Pte.	Watkins	L.

The Following were transferred and posted to "R" Battery

4030950	CQMS.	Rigby	E.	4040463	L/Cpl.	Gardner	K.	4036693	Sgt.	Bourne	C.
4039167	L/Cpl.	George	E.	4039893	Pte.	Arnold	L.	4040453	Pte.	Grosvenor	W.
4040331	Pte.	Bufton	A.	4104358	Pte.	Goodman	W.	4040352	Pte.	Bates	G.
4040491	Cpl.	Holliday	G.	4038357	L/Cpl.	Clarke	W.	4040501	Pte.	Hartshorne	A.
4040121	Pte.	Cadman	J.	4037112	Pte.	Harbidge	C.	4034615	Cpl.	Davies	R.
4039983	Pte.	Hipkiss	S.	4104939	Pte.	Daffurn	R.	4040260	L/Cpl.	Jones	S.
4040245	L/Cpl.	Eden	E.	4034163	Pte.	Jones	G.	4040443	Pte.	Foster	C.
4035619	L/Sgt.	Franklin	S.	4039603	Pte.	Jarrard	W.	5106754	Pte.	Fellowes	G.
4040005	Pte.	Kaines	P.	4037270	Cpl.	Gibbons	G.	4040174	Pte.	Lane	F.
4040236	Pte.	Grierson	D.	4040012	Cpl.	Lee	E.	4040456	Pte.	Gorman	H.
4038459	Pte.	Maiden	S.	4040454	Pte.	Gulliver	C.	4040587	Pte.	Miller	A.
4040302	Pte.	Hall	J.	4040579	Pte.	Montford	A.	4040499	Pte.	Hall	C.
4040291	Pte.	Neville	T. KIA	4038359	Pte.	Hall	F.	4040596	Pte.	Newton	L.
4040265	Pte.	Hayes	B.	4037359	L/Sgt.	Oliver	H.	4040164	Pte.	James	F.
4034979	Cpl.	Powell	E.	4040529	Pte.	Johnson	F.	5248531	L/Cpl.	Poole	F.
4040286	Pte.	Jeffries	G.	4040621	Pte.	Parsons	C.	4040162	Pte.	Jones	T.
4035952	Pte.	Rixon	R.	4033293	Sgt.	Philips	S.	803364	Pte.	Ritchie	N.

4039326	L/Cpl.	Ashton	C.	4040669	Pte.	Slater	T.	4039349	Pte.	Baker	H.
4040069	Pte.	Sheperd	A.	4039915	Pte.	Bodwell	A.	4040700	L/Cpl.	Winkle	J.
4039933	Pte.	Cartwright	T.	4040696	Pte.	Williams	B.	4040401	Pte.	Cowlishaw	F.
4040709	Pte.	Wright	W.	4039930	Pte.	Culliford	D.	4040088	Pte.	Worrall	E.
4040418	L/Sgt.	Darby	F.	4040090	Pte.	Wakely	P.	4040252	Pte.	Davies	E.
4040221	Pte.	Walker	H.	4040274	Pte.	Ellis	A.	4040729	Pte.	Wain	G.
4040137	Pte.	Fisher	J.	4040226	Pte.	Whitney	T.	4040451	Pte.	Fowler	F.
4040723	Pte.	Warburton	J.	4040732	Pte.	Yapp	W.	4040705	Pte.	Wooliscroft	T.
4040366	Pte.	Broomhall	P.	4040081	Pte.	Watkins	C.	4040363	L/Cpl.	Beardmore	J.
4040728	L/Cpl.	Walton	W.	4033068	Pte.	Carling	C.	4040231	Pte.	Youens	W.
4038939	Pte.	Clarke	H.	5046858	Pte.	Bourne	S.	4039927	Pte.	Cartwright	A.
4040355	L/Cpl.	Bamford	J.	4040427	Pte.	Davies	J.	4040109	Pte.	Blount	S.
4040414	Pte.	Dixon	B.	4039372	Pte.	Chance	W.	4040132	Pte.	Evans	W.
4039929	Pte.	Clee	W.	4031644	Pte.	Gould	S.	4040769	Pte.	Clay	J.
4039965	Pte.	Griffiths	W.	4040411	Pte.	Dale	T.	4039984	Pte.	Herbert	J.
4040135	Pte.	Edwards	C.	4040531	L/Cpl.	Jukes	H.	4040448	Pte.	Fisher	W.
4037323	Pte.	Jamieson	D.	4033066	Pte.	Griffiths	R.	4031467	Cpl.	Morriss	F.
4040500	Pte.	Horton	T.	4040627	Pte.	Pedley	L.	5107432	Pte.	Hickerton	J.
4040209	Pte.	Scott	J.	4039992	Pte.	Jones	A.	4040676	Pte.	Turvey	G.
4040557	Pte.	Lambert	D.	4040689	Pte.	Vaughan	E.	4040615	Pte.	Perry	L.
4038306	Pte.	Whittle	J.	4040066	Pte.	Skelton	H.	4040084	Pte.	Wright	G.
4040664	Pte.	Sanbrook	W.	4860684	Pte.	Coley	J.	4040217	Pte.	Thomas	C.
4040516	Pte.	Jones	H.	4040249	Pte.	Williams	W.	4040546	Pte.	Langley	J.
550095	Pte.	Western	G.	4035673	Cpl.	Lockley	W.	4040093	Pte.	Wharton	J.
4034350	Cpl.	Marks	C.	4039969	Pte.	Mayward	F.	406895	Pte.	Miller	C.
4040515	Pte.	Joiner	L.	4034357	Cpl.	Neale	T.	4040736	Pte.	Newall	T.
4039618	Pte.	O'Flynn	J.	4035688	Cpl.	Price	K.	4040622	L/Cpl.	Piper	W.
4040189	L/Cpl.	Parsons	F.	4040733	Pte.	Richards	R.	4040635	Pte.	Ratcliffe	F.
4040197	Pte.	Rock	E.	4040657	Pte.	Summers	F.	4105598	Cpl.	Webb	G.
4040224	Pte.	Wall	A.	4032348	Pte.	Wildon	A.	4040692	Pte.	Whittingham	E.
4040711	Pte.	Whent	H.								

The Following were transferred and posted to "S" Battery

4036550	CQMS	Page	W.	4039946	Pte.	Evans	E.	4040104	Pte.	Adams	J.
4040432	L/Cpl.	Edwards	A.	4040317	Pte.	Adams	A. KIA	4040437	Pte.	Foster	H.
4104643	Sgt.	Guy	G.	4040446	L/Cpl.	Fisher	V.	4040314	Pte.	Adams	F.
4039958	Pte.	Goast	H.	4040322	L/Cpl.	Astle	W.	4039959	Pte.	Griffin	C.
4039889	Pte.	Armstrong	J. KIA	4040465	Pte.	Griffiths	L.	4040320	Pte.	Averill	S.
4039955	Pte.	Greenwood	J.	4039912	Pte.	Barker	T.	4040145	Pte.	Gwatkin	G.
4040365	Pte.	Blyde	E.	4040484	Pte.	Harding	J.	4039917	Pte.	Beard	G.
4035999	Cpl.	Harriss	A.	4040110	Cpl.	Bentley	J.	4039974	Pte.	Harriss	C.
4037794	Pte.	Barnett	W.	4040478	Pte.	Huyton	T.	4040105	Pte.	Billingham	J.
4040341	Pte.	Bradley	F.	4040495	Pte.	Horton	H.	4040339	Pte.	Bentley	A.
4032714	Pte.	Hooton	J.	4038936	Pte.	Barton	W.	4040511	Pte.	Harriss	S.
4035707	Pte.	Cornes	R.	4040141	Pte.	Gay	R.	4039931	Pte.	Cartwright	S.
4039934	Pte.	Collins	E.	4040158	Pte.	Jeromes	S.	4039937	Pte.	Cudd	H.
4040519	Pte.	Jackson	W.	4040118	Pte.	Chamberlain	F.	4040519	Pte.	Jackson	W.
4040383	Pte.	Clarke	J.	4040543	Pte.	Kenworthy	D.	4040308	Pte.	Crowe	H.
4040306	Pte.	Lane	L.	4040609	Pte.	Powell	J.	4040015	Pte.	Lewis	P.

No.	Rank	Name		No.	Rank	Name		No.	Rank	Name	
4040629	Pte.	Potter	J.	4037349	Cpl.	Maslin	G.	4040608	Pte.	Perry	R.
4040568	Cpl.	Mottram	E.	4040192	Pte.	Pugh	R.	4037357	Cpl.	Nichols	J.
4040192	Pte.	Pugh	R.	4037357	Cpl.	Nichols	J.	4040625	Pte.	Powell	E.
4040597	L/Cpl.	Owen	J.	6971000	L/Sgt.	Robley	B.	4040361	Pte.	Brookes	J.
4040637	Pte.	Roberts	H.	4039908	Pte.	Brown	A.	4040297	Pte.	Slater	T.
4039936	Pte.	Colwell	D.	4040064	Pte.	Symes	C.	4040381	Pte.	Cotton	S.
4040316	Pte.	Allan	R.	4040244	Pte.	Cutts	G.	4040262	Pte.	Aspley	G. MM
4040380	L/Cpl.	Causer	F.	4040324	Pte.	Beard	N.	4040376	Pte.	Chetta	F.
4040116	Pte.	Broughton	G.	4040386	Pte.	Collingwood	R.	4036887	Cpl.	Boughey	S.
4040433	Pte.	Edwards	A.	4040327	L/Cpl.	Brookes	E.	4134570	Pte.	Evans	W. KIA
4040235	Pte.	Butler	G.	4039948	Pte.	Edwards	G KAS	4040235	Pte.	Butler	G.
4040051	Pte.	Franklin	R.	4040232	Pte.	Barker	S.	4040449	Pte.	Fitzmaurice	F.
4040410	Pte.	Horne	A.	4040458	L/Sgt.	Gray	W.	4040508	Pte.	Harrison	J.
4039963	Pte.	Guy	D.	4039982	Pte.	Hill	R.	4039966	Pte.	Godfrey	W.
4037293	Pte.	Hassall	S.	4040549	Pte.	Greenway	R.	4040234	Pte.	Humphries	R.
4036655	Pte.	Griffiths	J.	4040146	Pte.	Hutchinson	T.	4039994	Pte.	Jones	H.
4040480	Pte.	Hill	D.	4040161	Pte.	Jennings	N. MM	4039990	Pte.	Jinks	W.
4040167	Pte.	Kirk	N.	4040535	Pte.	Jones	J.	4040548	Pte.	Lampitt	W.
4039993	Pte.	Jervis	E.	4032338	Pte.	Lewis	C.	4040031	Pte.	Nelson	H.
4036662	Cpl.	Onions	J.	4040570	Pte.	Mathias	J.	4040648	Pte.	Smith	S.
4040614	Pte.	Pearce	J.	4037395	Pte.	Sandford	F.	4040606	Pte.	Poole	G.
4040246	Pte.	Summers	L.	4039260	Pte.	Payne	S.	5835876	Pte.	Swain	P.
4040623	Pte.	Powmer	S.	4038525	Pte.	Tunnicliffe	C.	4040613	Pte.	Plimmer	S.
4040216	Pte.	Talbot	1.	4040187	Pte.	Phelps	S.	4035735	Pte.	Tudor	W.
4040194	Pte.	Rice	W.	4040092	Pte.	Wooley	1. KIA	4040193	L/Cpl.	Rowen	R.
4040097	Pte.	Ward	J.	4040645	Pte.	Sloan	R.	4040718	Cpl.	Walton	A.
4040667	Cpl.	Snape	A.	4207630	Pte.	White	B.	4040179	Pte.	Slater	F.
4040722	Pte.	Wood	H.	4031727	Pte.	Thompson	A.	4040321	Pte.	Abbiss	A.
4032855	Pte.	Thomas	G.	4039903	Pte.	Boden	S.	4040213	Pte.	Turner	A.
4040683	L/Cpl.	Titley	A.	4040305	Pte.	Williams	N.	4040646	Pte.	Slater	J.
4040076	Pte.	Widlake	H.	4037189	Pte.	Staley	H.	4035991	L/Sgt.	Walker	I.
4040101	L/Cpl.	Youens	C.	4040223	Pte.	Watson	J.	4040343	Pte.	Bull	T.
4040222	Pte.	Warder	S.	4040384	Pte.	Cotterill W.					

The following have not joined for the following reasons:

4040216	Pte.	Talbot	J.	Addmitted, Bracebridge hospital. 11/02/42.
4040133	Pte.	Evans	T.	Addmitted, Louth Infirmary 19/02/42.
4040657	Pte.	Summers	T.	Addmitted, Bracebridge hospital 25/02/42.
4040352	Pte.	Bates	G.}	
4860684	Pte.	Coley	J.}	Attending course at ROAC. workshops Liecs.
4039969	Pte.	Hayward	F.}	
4035629	L/Sgt	Franklin	S.	Attached 70th. Bn. KOYLI.
4040236	Pte.	Grierson	T.}	
4040286	Pte.	Maiden	S.}	Attached 30th. East Yorkshire Regt.
4032348	Pte.	Wilden	A.}	
4040274	Pte.	Ellis	W.	On Leave 03/03/42
4040234	Pte.	Humphries	A.	Attached 227 Fd. Park Coy. RE.

Appendix 14

DISPOSITION OF OFFICERS
11TH MARCH 1942

Regimental HQ.

Lt.Col. EO. Herbert C/O
Capt. Corbett
MTO.Lieut. Jones (att.'S'Batt)
Lieut. QM. Lock
2/Lt. Raitz
2/Lt. Sturley
2/Lt. Meredith

'Q' Battery,

Major JA.Hill C/O
Capt. Martin
Capt. Moorshead
Lieut. Down
Lieut. Browne
2/Lt. Stokes

R Battery

Major FL Justice C/O
Capt. Maurice
Capt. Noyes
2/Lt. Prutton
2/Lt. Gibbons

S Battery

Major TL. Lawrence C/O
Capt. Shields
Capt. Dyas
Capt. Cory-Wright
Capt. Bristowe
Lieut. McCowan
2/Lt. Shaw
2/Lt. Hughes

2/Lt. Forster
2/Lt. Mulholland
2/Lt. Parkin
2/Lt. Jacques
2/Lt. Walton
2/Lt. Hyne
2/Lt. Paddock

Disposition of W.O's and Sergeants

Regimental HQ	'Q' Battery	R Battery	S Battery
RSM. Ayling	TSM/BSM. Ford	TSM/BSM. Cook	BQMS Page.
BQMS.Anderson	BSM. Morton	BSM. Woodcock	BSM. Read
Sgt. Henley	BQMS. Norcress	BSM. Barnes	Sgt. Lewis
" Palmer	Sgt. Lindup	BQMS. Rigby	" Hunt
" Furlong	" McGoldrich	Sgt. Patterson	" Cox
" Rushbrook	" Davidson	" Layton	
" Clacher	" Bourne	" Owen	
" Fleming	" Floyd		
" Winter	" Philips		

Appendix 15

DISPOSITION OF BOMBARDIERS
AND LANCE BOMBARDIERS

Regimental HQ.		'Q' Battery		R Battery		S Battery	
Bdrs.	Roberts (39)	Bdrs.	Davies	Bdrs.	Bennett	Bdrs.	Boughey
	Howells		Holliday		Cowern		Bentley
L/Bdrs	Brookes		Knight		Chataway		Cordell
	Marklew		Lee		Edwards		Gibbons
			Marks		Fletcher		Harriss
			Morriss		Grimshaw		Hollaway
			Price		Ingram		Maslin
			Powell		Jeffries (91)		Mottram
			Webb		Linard		Mountford
		L/Bdrs	Ashton		Lockley		Nichols
			Ebdy		Neale		Onions
			Eden		Powis		Snape
			Gardner		Tunnicliffe		Walton
			George	L/Bdrs	Bamford	L/Bdrs	Astle
			Jones (60)		Beardmore		Causer
			Moyle		Clee		Edwards
			Poole		Clarke		Fisher
			Shelley		Jukes		Handley
					Lewis		Owen
					Mason		Parsons
					Pipe		Rowen
					Price		Titley
					Poutney		Winkle
					Walton		Youens

15TH SCOTTISH DIVISION ORDER OF BATTLE
26TH JUNE 1944 HQ 15TH SCOTTISH DIVISION

HQ. 44th Lowland Inf. Bde.
8th Royal Scots
6th Royal Scots Fusiliers
6th King's Own Scottish Borderers

HQ 46th Highland Inf. Bde.
9th Cameronians
2nd Glasgow Highlanders
7th Seaforth Highlanders

HQ 227th Highland Inf. Bde.
10th Highland Light Infantry
2nd Gordon Highlanders
2nd Argyll & Sutherland Highlanders

Royal Army Service Corps
62nd Company
283rd Company
284th Company

Royal Army Medical corps
153rd Field Ambulance
193rd Field Ambulance
194th Field Ambulance
40th Field Hygiene section
22nd Field Dressing Station
23rd Field Dressing Station

Royal Electrical & Mechanical Engineers
44th Lowland Inf. Bde. Workshops
46th Highland Inf. Bde. Workshops
227th Highland Inf. Bde. Workshops
15th Infantry Workshops

Machine Gun Regiment
1st Middlesex Regt.

Recce. Regiment
15th Scottish Recce Regt.

Royal Artillery
131st Field Regiment R.A.
181st Field Regiment R.A. (6 KSLI)
190th Field Regiment R.A.
97th Anti - Tank Regiment RA.
119th Light Anti - Aircraft Regt. R.A.

Royal Engineers
20th Field Company
278th Field Company
279th Field Company
624th Field Company

Provost Company
15th Scottish Div.
Provost Coy. C.M.P

Intelligence Corps
39th Field Security Section

Ordnance
15th Ordnance Field Park
305th M.L and B.U.

This order of battle survived the period of the campaign except:
97th Anti-Tank Regt. RA. were replaced by 102nd Anti -Tank Regt. R.A. Northumberland Hussars
22nd Field Dressing Station transferred to 8th Corps Troops March 1945

At the end of the War, the Division had lost almost 12,000 men, including almost 2,000 killed.

Brigades

44th Inf. Bde.	03/09/39 - 31/08/45
45th Inf. Bde.	03/09/39 - 05/01/43
46th Inf. Bde.	03/09/39 - 31/08/45
227th Inf. Bde.	10/09/43 - 31/08/45
6th Gds. Tank. Bde.	04/01/43 - 14/01/43

Higher Formations Served Under

Scottish Command	03/09/39 - 03/05/40
Southern Command	04/05/40 - 20/05/40
Eastern Command	21/05/40 - 04/06/40
11 Corps	05/06/40 - 20/11/41
9 Corps	21/11/41 - 30/11/41
9 Corps District	01/12/41 - 28/09/42
Northumbrian District	29/09/42 -12/04/43
1 Corps	13/04/43 -19/06/43
8 Corps	20/06/43 - 23/07/44
30 Corps	23/07/44 - 29/07/44
8 Corps	30/07/44 -14/08/44
12 Corps	15/08/44 - 04/10/44
8 Corps	05/10/44 - 24/10/44
12 Corps	25/10/44 - 31/10/44
8 Corps	01/11/44 - 27/01/45
30 Corps	28/01/45 - 25/02/45
1st Canadian Army	26/02/45 - 06/03/45
12 Corps	07/03/45 - 04/04/45
8 Corps	05/04/45 - 31/08/45

Theatres of War

United Kingdom	North West Europe
03/09/39 - 13/06/44	14/06/44 - 31/08/45

Battles
1944

26th June - 2nd July	The Odon
4th July -18th July	Caen
30th July - 9th August	Mont Pincon
17th Sept - 27th Sept	The Nederrijn

1945

8th Feb -10th March	The Rhineland
23rd March - 27th April	The Rhine

Appendix 17

DISPOSITION OF OFFICERS IN
THE EUROPEAN THEATRE

178 Battery

Maj.	R. Moorshead	Battery Commander (June - Sept. 1944)
Maj.	R. Walters	Battery Commander
Maj.	Sharpe	Battery Commander
Maj.	GC. Grahame	Battery Commander
Maj.	P. Attewell	Battery Commander
Capt.	J. Meredith	C Troop Commander (later Battery Commander)
Capt.	ADG. Shaw	D Troop Commander
Capt.	ACMP. Ducquenoy	Command Post Officer
Capt.	R. Foulds	Command Post Officer
Lieut.	Hargreaves	Command Post Officer (wounded in Normandy)
Lieut.	P. Clements	Gun Position Officer
Lieut.	R. Todd	Gun Position Officer
Lieut.	A. Mcloed	Signals Officer
Lieut.	R. Gow	Gun Position Officer
B.S.M.	Cooke	C Troop
B.S.M.	Wheeler	C Troop
B.S.M.	Oliver	D Troop

179 Battery

Maj.	RA. Gorle	Battery Commander
Maj.	T. Sedgwicke	Battery Commander (wounded in Normandy)
Maj.	J. Robertson	Battery Commander (end of hostilities)
Capt.	JS. Cunis	E Troop Commander (later Battery Commander)
Capt.	N. Prutton	F Troop Commander
Capt.	G. Easter	Battery Commander
Lieut.	P. Mulholland	Command Post Officer
Lieut.	M. Walters	Gun Position Officer
Lieut.	J. Boyd	Gun Position Officer/ Troop Capt (E Troop)
Lieut.	D. Small	E Troop Leader / Gun Position Officer
Ueut.	EWK. Jones	Command Post Officer
Lieut.	RJ. Hewitt	Command Post Officer
Lieut.	Murray	Command PostOfficer
B.S.M.	Milner	Battery Sergeant Major

177 Battery

Maj.	A. Browne	Battery Commander
Capt.	J. Cory-Wright	A Troop Commander KIA. Normandy
Capt.	TJ. Stokes	B Troop Commander
B.S.M.	Clacker	"B' Troop Sgt. Major
Lieut.	Wright	

Appendix 18

178 BTY / 181 FIELD REGT.
R.A. GUN POSITIONS

Country & Date	Position	Comments
UK/FRANCE		
June 1944		
11th	Left Worthing	
13th	Embarked King George V Dock	
15th	Disembarked, Arrowmanches	
17th	Brecy	Divisional Conc. Area
25th	Brouay, Lost A Sub Gun	Sgt.Gunn, Gnr's McMorland
	in first action	and Wheaton all killed
27th	Cheux, Haut de Bosque	
July 1944		
2nd	Sequeville	Mine-Fields
5th	St. Mauvieux	Lost Hawin and Walker
		seriously wounded
12th	Mouen/Everecy/Estry	
20th	Balleroy	American Sector
28th	Caumont	OP. took direct hit.
29th	St.Martin de Bescances	Div. Comdr. wounded
30th	Les Loges	
August 1944		
3rd	St.Denis/Beny-Bocage	
5th	Bretville-sur-Odon	
	Charles de Percy.	
10th	Estry	
11th	Monchamp	
14th	Foret de Anglais	Plagued by mosquitoes
21st	Near Falaise	
24th	Le Neuborg, passing through	The chase through France
	Bernay and Orbec	and Belgium
26th	Louviers	
27th	Night crossing of the Seine	Met little opposition
September 1944		
5th	Beauvais	lots of German prisoners

BELGIUM

September 1944

6th	Lille	crossed French border
7th	Harlebeke	
10th	Hom-Beek	Sgt.Fletchers MG.post
12th	Arrived Albert Canal	
14th	Gheel- Bridgehead	Lost Adams 17, Adams 05 Evans 33 all killed. Gnr's Russell, Broomhall, Jackson, Lt. Hargreaves all wounded.
17th	Moll	

HOLLAND

September 1944

20th	Eindhoven	
23rd	Best	Glider position.
25th	St.Odenroede	

October 1944

1st	Beek & Donk	Overhaul
8th	Overloon/ Venray	In support 3rd Division
14th	Beek & Donk	Rest.
16th	Looshook	S'Hertogonbosch Sector.
18th	Best	Harboured.
20th	North-East of Best	Advance along Canal
22nd	Tilburg	Tilburg liberated.
27th	Asten	Battle to stem enemy counter attack from Venlo.

Nov

7th	Niercant / Meijel	Minefields
25th	Horst	
30th	Maasbree	Blerick taken Xmas & New years Day.

December 1944

	Stuck on the River Maas

January 1945

10th	Duerne	Overhaul and rest.
17th	Maejyck	In support 7th Armd. Division.
24th	Tilburg	Rest and Refit

February 1945

4th	Nijmegen	Harboured.
6th	Groesbeek	
8th	Kraenburg	Sgt's Gibbons and Darby wounded
18th	Bedburg	Bombed - Jet planes!

March 1945

1st	Tilburg	Rest and Refit
6th	Lummell/Belgium	Training for crossing the Rhine
25th	Rhine crossing/Xanten	Assault crossing 0200 Hrs, Regt shelled and bombed!

GERMANY

April 1945

14th	Holdenstadt	Strong SS position at Ueltzen
17th	Molzen	
27th	Breitlingen	River Elbe Assault.
30th	Artlingen	River Elbe crossing 2300 hrs

May 1945

1st	Gulzow	5 enemy planes shot down, after being bombed by ME 262
2nd	Hamwarde	Shelled and bombed, One casualty Bdr Brooker 179 Bty.
4th	Vorburg-News of surrender	178 Bty in action for last time
5th	Bargteheide	Regt. Harboured
6th	Bargteheide	Regt.in Conc.area to await occupational duties

Appendix 19

FIELD RETURN OF OFFICERS

Week Ending 12th. February 1944

Army No	Substantive Rank	Higher or temp. Rank Held	Name & Initials		Date taken on Strength	Appointment
37198	Major	T/L/Col.	Deveruex	ACE.	06/08/42	C/O.
49828	Captain	T/Major	Grahame	GR.	21/05/43	2 I/C.
89585	Captain	T/Major	Moorshead	RM.	11/03/42	Bty. Comm.
58015	Captain	T/Major	Browne	ARS.	26/05/43	Bty. Comm.
58020	Captain	T/Major	Sedgwick	WT.	10/09/43	Bty. Comm.
137103	Captain		Cunis	AS.	27/08/43	
70745	Captain		Attewell	GP.	10/01/44	
122263	Lieut.	T/Captain	Martin	JL.	01/03142*	
122236	Lieut.	T/Captain	Bristowe	RG.	01/03/42*	
72690	Lieut.	T/Captain	Cory-Wright	AJJ.	08/03/42	
164853	Lieut.	T/Captain	Shaw	ADG.	01/03/42*	
212809	Lieut.	T/Captain	Matthews	GW.	29/06/42	Adjutant.
177831	Lieut.	T/Capt.	Meredith	J.	01/03/42*	
136684	Lieut.	T/Captain	Prutton	NW.	01/03142*	
52523	Lieut.	T/Captain	Newberry	CE.	22/09/43	
244788	Lieut(QM)		Shaw	JT.	20/08/43	
137254	Lieut.		MacOwen	DN.	01/03/42*	
276951	Lieut.		Munro	GD.	15/05/43	
193462	Lieut.		Cook	HD.	15/04/43	
187117	Lieut.		Stokes	JT.	01/03/42*	
268766	Lieut.		Whipp	FE.	03/08/43	
249956	Lieut		Hargreaves	JR.	07/11/42	
227092	Lieut.		Trewby	DFA.	05/04/42*	
200938	Lieut.		Ward	RB.	09/09/43	
276693	Lieut.		Buchanan	HS.	29/05/43	
273200	Lieut.		McLeod	A.	01/08/43	
186476	Lieut.		Ducquenoy	ACMP.	10/01/44	
187118	Lieut.		Walters	MJA.	01/03/42*	
204406	Lieut.		Mulholland	P.	01/03/42*	
167234	Lieut.		Boyd	JH.	20/01/43	
10311S	Lieut.		Jones	EWK	10/03/42	
271505	Lieut.		Hewitt	RW.	24/04/43	
267970	Lieut.		Porter	JP.	15/05/43	
229091	Lieut.		Thomlinson	JW.	05/04/42	
293403	Lieut.		Gow	RF.	18/09/43	
289961	Lieut.		Livie	RR.	28/08/43	
252688	Captain (RAMC)		Lowden	CRS.	23/04/43	Medical Officer
133934	Lieut.		Jones	11.	20/09/42	

132421	Lieut.		Logan	J.	15/11/43	
272486	2/Lieut.		Smith	D.	04/09/43	
293417	2/Lieut.		Murray	JPME	18/09/43	
293767	2/Lieut.		Fraser	D.	25/09/43	
293771	2/Lieut.		Muir	EN.	25/09/43	
293780	2/Lieut.		Christie	JMcG.	25/09/43	
302590	2/Lieut.		Clarke	CT.	11/12/43	
302956	2/Lieut.		Nye	SGN.	11/12/43	
302813	2/Lieut.		Kinsler	E.	18/12/43	
302827	2/Lieut.		Corns	JR.	18/12/43	

*All Ex-KSLI Officers

Week Ending 7th. April 1945

38398	Major	T/L/Col.	Keene	TP.	06/03/45	C/O.
44862	Captain	T/Major	Gorle	RA.	09/09/44	2 I/C.
49828	Captain	T/Major	Grahame	GC.	21/05/43	Bty. Comm. 178
58015	Captain	T/Major	Browne	ARS.	04/05/43	Bty. Comm. 177
88108	Captain	T/Major	Robertson	J.	19/12/44	Bty. Comm. 179
62418	Captain		Sharp	SH.	05/04/44	
137103	Captain		Cunis	JS.	27/03/43	
212809	Lieut.	T/Capt.	Bristowe	RG.	01/03/42*	
164853	Lieut.	T/Capt.	Shaw	ADG.	01/03/42*	
156684	Lieut.	T/Capt.	Prutton	NW.	01/03/42*	
212809	Lieut.	T/Capt.	Matthews	GW.	24/08/42	
276951	Lieut	T/Capt.	Munro	GD.	08/11/44	
177831	Lieut.	T/Capt.	Meredith	J.	01/03/42*	
89823	Lieut.	T/Capt.	Wilcock	RJE.	29/11/44	
285922	Lieut.		McWilliams	JW.	13/12/44	
167234	Lieut.		Boyd	JH.	21/08/44	
244788	Lieut. (QM)		Shaw	JT.	20/08/43	
174601	Lieut.		Tyrer	JM.	30/09/44	
186476	Lieut.		Ducquenoy	ACMP.	10/04/44	
187118	Lieut.		Walters	MJA.	28/06/44	
229091	Lieut.		Thomlinson	JH.	05/04/42	
223092	Lieut.		Trewby	DFA.	03/04/42	
143462	Lieut.		Cook	AD.	10/04/43	
268766	Lieut.		Whipp	FE.	03/08/43	
271505	Lieut.		Hewett	RW.	24/04/43	
273200	Lieut.		McLeod	A.	01/03/42*	
273992	Lieut.		Foulds	RA.	30/09/44	
289961	Lieut.		Livie	RR.	28/07/43	
293417	Lieut.		Murray	JP.	18/09/43	
219905	Lieut.		Mitchell	JE.	27/07/44	
302827	Lieut.		Corns	JR.	02/09/44	
308306	Lieut.		Wright	CP.	01/08/44	
271543	Lieut.		Marsh	MC.	04/02/45	
187118	Lieut.		Stokes	TJ.	05/03/45	
249936	Lieut.		Hargreaves	JR.	05/03/45	

293403	Lieut.	Gow	RF.	05/03/45
305685	Lieut.	Livingstone	SV.	31/03/45
	Lieut.	Small	DJ.	21/12/44
	Lieut.	Easter	GE.	02/01/45
	Lieut.	Martin	DE.	21/04/45
204406	Lieut.	Mulholland	P.	01/03/42
302596	Lieut.	Nye	SEN.	11/12/45
70745	Capt.	Attewell	GP.	10/01/44
200938	T/Capt.	Ward	RB.	09/09/43
137254	Lieut.	MacOwen	DN	01/03/42*
103115	T/Capt.	Jones	EWK	10/03/42
	Lieut.	Porter	JP.	

*All Ex-KSLI Officers

Appendix 20

NAMES, RANK AND FINAL DISPOSITION
OF THE OFFICERS AND MEN OF C TROOP
AT THE END OF THE WAR:

The following is a list that was taken from one of the many notebooks kept by Major John Meredith, it contains the names, rank and final disposition of the Officers and men of C Troop at the end of the war:

SEAC*   South East Asia Command

Pickfords.   Young Soldiers sent to Far East to relieve Troops

Rank	Name	Disposition	Month	Year
Bty.Sgt.Majors	Cook	Demobbed	August	1945
	Wheeler	Posted RHQ	May	1945
Bty.Sgt's	Dodd	AIG. Course	November	1944
	Gunn	K.l.A.	July	1944
	Darby	To 121 LAA	January	1946
	Gibbons	To 121 LAA	January	1946
	Fletcher	To 121 LAA	January	1946
	Young	To 121 LAA	January	1946
Fitter/Gunner				
Bdr.	Kilby	Posted Pickfords*	June	1945
Driver/Mech				
L/Bdr.	Hickerton	To Hospital	March	1945
Gnr.	Jones 92	Demobbed	December	1945
"	Lewis	Posted Pickfords*	June	1945
"	Williams	Posted 5 RHA	October	1945
"	Ball	Demobbed	October	1945
"	Postlemont	Posted SEAC	October	1945
"	McInerey	Posted SEAC	August	1945
"	Lewis	Posted 4 RHA	January	1946
"	Newton	Posted 121 I AA	January	1946
Driver/Operators				
L/Bdr.	Hassall	Posted 121 LAA	January	1946
Gnr	Abbis	Posted 121 LAA	January	1946
"	Edwards	Demobbed	December	1945
"	Whittingham	To Hospital	Nervous Exhaustion	
"	Lees	Posted HQ. RA.		
Bdr.	Brannan	Demobbed	September	1945
Gnr	Woods	Demobbed	December	1945
"	Watts	Posted SEAC	July	1945

Vehicle Mechanic

L/Bdr.	Fowler	Demobbed	December	1945

G.P.O. Acks

L/Sgt	Mottram	Posted 51 Hvy/Rgt.	January	1946
Gnr	Barnes	Posted 121 LAA	January	1946
"	Tomkiss	Posted Away	January	1945
"	Healy	posted Bn. H/Q.	April	1946

Signallers

Gnr	Jackson	Posted 121 LAA	January	1946
"	Braithwaite	B Release	October	1945
"	Cotton	Demobbed	December	1945
"	Huyton	Class B Release	December	1945
"	Mawes	Posted 5 RHA	October	1945
"	Russell	Posted Pickfords*	May	1945
"	Murray	Posted 'Xainy?'	June	1945
"	Baker	Posted 121 LAA	January	1946
"	Watson	Demobbed	December	1945
"	Holland	Posted RHQ	June	1945
"	Mountford	Posted RHQ	June	1945

L.M.G./Piat

Gnr.	Curtis	Wounded	July	1944
"	Smith	Wounded	December	1944

Gunners

L/Sgt.	Eden	Demobbed	December	1945
Bdr.	Forknall	Demobbed	December	1945
"	Dalton	Wounded	July	1944
"	Packer	Posted to Infantry	December	1944
"	Goodson	Graded 'B6'	January	1945
"	Hughes	Posted SEAC	July	1945
"	Anderson	Posted RASC	July	1945
L/Bdr	Rowlands	Posted SEAC	August	1945
"	Hughes	Posted 121 LAA	January	1946
"	Smith	Posted 5 RHA	October	1945
Gnr.	May	Wounded	July	1944
"	Wheaton	K.I.A.	July	1944
"	Parsons	Posted SEAC	October	1945
Gnr.	**NEAL**	**Demobbed**	**December**	**1945**
"	Willey	Posted SEAC	August	1945
"	Adams 17	K.I.A.	September	1944
"	Adams 05	K.I.A.	September	1944
"	Evans 33	K.I.A.	September	1944
"	McMorland	K.I.A.	July	1944
"	Plummer	Posted to Infantry	December	1944
"	Meston	Posted SEAC	August	1945
"	Hall 59	Posted 121 LM	January	1946

"	Hawin	Wounded	August	1944
"	Beardmore	Posted Rgt.HQ.	December	1945
"	Edwards	Demobbed	December	1945
"	Roberts	Posted RASC	June	1945
"	Chambers	Posted to Infantry	December	1944
"	Randle	Posted SEAC	August	1945
"	Hardy	Surveyors Course	October	1944
"	Walker	Wounded	August	1944
"	Lee	see driver I/C		
"	Smith	From 50th Div	January	1946
"	Dantry	"	"	"
"	Morriss	"	"	"
"	Little	"	"	"
L/Bdr	Brydon	Demobbed	December	1945
Drivers I/C				
L/Bdr.	Airey	Posted 5 RHA	October	1945
Gnr	Cotton 17	Posted Pickfords*	May	1945
"	Compton	Posted Pickfords*	May	1945
"	Davis 08	Posted to Infantry	December	1944
"	Mills	Posted SEAC	August	1945
"	Morriss	Posted RASC	August	1945
"	Williams	B Release	October	1945
"	Lee	To Gun Sub at own request		
"	Hanbury	To Bty. HQ.		
"	Newton	To Dvr/Mech.		
"	Adams	To 121 LAA	January	1946
"	Jervis	To 121 LAA	January	1946
"	Harrison	Demobbed	December	1945
"	Lee	Posted SEAC	August	1945
Observation Post Ack.				
Bdr.	Aspley MM.	Posted 5 RHA	November	1945
Cooks				
Pte.	Hood (attached)	To Bty HQ	Hospital - Burns	
"	Brown	Posted Course		

Appendix 21

C TROOP CASUALTIES DURING WORLD WAR II

C Troop Casualties

	Killed	Wounded	Died	Evacuated Sick
Officers	-	5	-	-
Other Ranks	6	14	-	2

Personnel Wounded and left Troop

Bdr.	Dalton	Discharged
Gnr	May	Discharged
"	Curtis	Depot
"	Hawin	Depot
"	Walker	Still in Hospital Dec 1944
"	Broomhall	Depot
"	Smith 63	Ward 15 Br.General Hospital BLA
"	Whittingham	Discharged

Personnel Wounded and returned to Troop

Gnr	Huyton	Shrapnel in elbow/remained with unit
"	Russell	Nervous Exhaustion, evacuated 4 days
"	Jackson	Hand wound, evacuated 14 days
"	Lewis	Lacerations & shock, remained with unit
Sgt	Darby	Head wound, skull fracture, evacuated
"	Gibbons	Head wound, evacuated 14 days

Troop Officers

Capt	J. Meredith	Troop Commander/wounded 16/9/44
Lieut	D.P. D'Ambruiel	GPO/wounded July. 1944 posted HQ.RA
"	A.C.M.P. Ducquenoy	Troop Leader/GPO,Posted 20 Laa Jan. 1946
"	M. Walters	Troop Leader/GPO, posted to 179 Bty.
"	S. Nye	Troop Leader/CPO, Wounded Aug.1944
"	R. Hargreaves	Troop Leader/CPO, Wounded Sep. 1944
"	R. Foulds	Troop Leader/CPO, Posted SEAC Aug 1944
Capt.	T.J. Stokes	Troop Commander,to177 Bty June 1944
"	J. Meredith	T/C. to 71 LAA. Jan 1946, Demobbed Feb. 1946

Appendix 22

PERSONNEL RECOMMENDED FOR AWARDS
178 BTY. 181 FIELD REGT. R.A.

Personnel Recommended for Honours	Recommended Award	Date	Actual Award
Bdr. G. Aspley	Military Medal	July 1944	December 1945
" "	" "	Sep 1944	Military Medal
Gnr P. Broomhall	Military Medal	July 1944	M.l.D.
" "	" "	Sep 1944	June 1945
Bdr. C.Brannan	Military Medal	Dec 1944	C.in C's Cert*
Gnr. Jackson	Military Medal	Feb 1945	C.in C's Cert
L/Bdr. A.Smith 88	Div.Comm.Cert.	Dec 1944	C.in C's Cert

Those Killed In Action with 178 Battery

Sgt.	Arthur Gunn	25th June 1944 }	
Gnr.	Ralph McMorland	25th June 1944 }	First day in action.
"	Stanley Wheaton	25th June 1944 }	
L/Bdr.	Richard Poutney	17th July 1944	
Gnr	James Evans	17th Sept 1944	
"	John Adams(05)	17th Sept 1944	
"	Alfred Adams(17)	18th Sept 1944	
"	Frederick Mills(81)	5th Dec 1944	
"	William Evans	25th Mar 1945	
Bdr.	Edward Evans(58)	12th April 1945	
Gnr.	James Forrest	9th. May 1945	

Batmen

Gnr.	Balcombe	Posted SEAC	Aug 1945
"	Rawlings	Posted Home Forces	July 1945
"	Bulling	Demobbed	July 1945

*C.in C's Cert. Commander in Chief's Certificate

INDEX OF FORMATION & UNITS

INDEX OF PLACE NAMES

INDEX OF NAMES

Stokes, Capt. TJ. 14, 15, 43, 58
Student, Gen. 21
Sturley, 2/Lt. L.A. 5, 42

Titley, L/Cpl.A. 4
Thomlinson, Capt.P 14,23,28
Tudor, Gnr. W. 4, 41

Wainwright Brig. 7
Walters, 2/Lt. MJA. 4, 5, 43
Wheaton, Gnr. 16, 18
Wissing, Unteroffizer. 3
Woolcombe, Capt. R. 16, 22
Wright, Lt. JC 42

N.B. Ranks shown are the highest held with the unit.